Continuous Strand Weaving For Beginners:
On 5ft and 6ft Triangle Looms

2nd Edition

Theresa Jewell and Ashli Couch
Stoney Meadow Alpacas and Stone Mountain Looms
Holley, New York

Contents

Introduction

We've finally did it. We finally put our talents together to bring you an instructional pattern book for continuous strand weaving. Go ahead and skip to the good stuff, or stick around and learn a little bit about your instructors.

Theresa Jewell started this fabulous past time in 2003. She first started out trying to find something to do with all her alpaca fiber from her animals. Of course there was crocheting, knitting, and spinning, but she wanted more. She spent a lot of time researching and trying different techniques before she finally discovered her passion for the frame looms.

The frame looms appealed to her for a few reasons. First, there is no setup. That's right! NO SET UP! You slip on your slipknot and begin weaving right away. The open weave also appealed to her because it was different and unique. Not to mention the open weave makes the piece of fabric lay beautifully. And finally, because it was something she could do right in her home with her fluffy alpaca or, as she fondly calls them, her yarn babies.

It took several years of hard work and learning before Theresa's dreams were met. In 2017 Theresa and her husband, Chuck Jewell, were able to purchase Stone Mountain Looms from Don and Penny McNeil.

This is where I come in. I happened to be best friends with Theresa's niece and somehow always managed to be over at her house growing up. As a result, I adopted her as my aunt and also my awesome yarn buddy.

She started me out on one of her rectangle looms at a demonstration and the rest is history. It always seemed to be on fly with a large audience when Theresa suckered me into trying another fantastic yarn craft. I learned to weave on the frame loom, the peg loom, and how to spin fiber on a spinning wheel at different demonstrations from 2013 to 2017. Now I own eleven looms and travel with Theresa to teach classes and introduce more yarn lovers to her wonderful looms.

One faithful day, while at an alpaca show, the subject of books came up. I happen to write fantasy romance fiction in my spare time and have a degree in history. Sharing this knowledge with Theresa got us thinking. Why not use my writing abilities and publishing knowledge with her weaving patterns, looms, and knowledge to produce something magical?

So here we are, working together to give you our first continuous strand loom weaving on a frame loom book. And don't worry, we already have about ten more planned!

-Ashli

Introduction 2

Welcome to our 2nd edition! We've fixed our mistakes, added photographs for ALL of our patterns, and added some new patterns. We cannot wait for you to get started on your 5ft and 6ft Triangle looms.

Enjoy,
-Ashli and Theresa

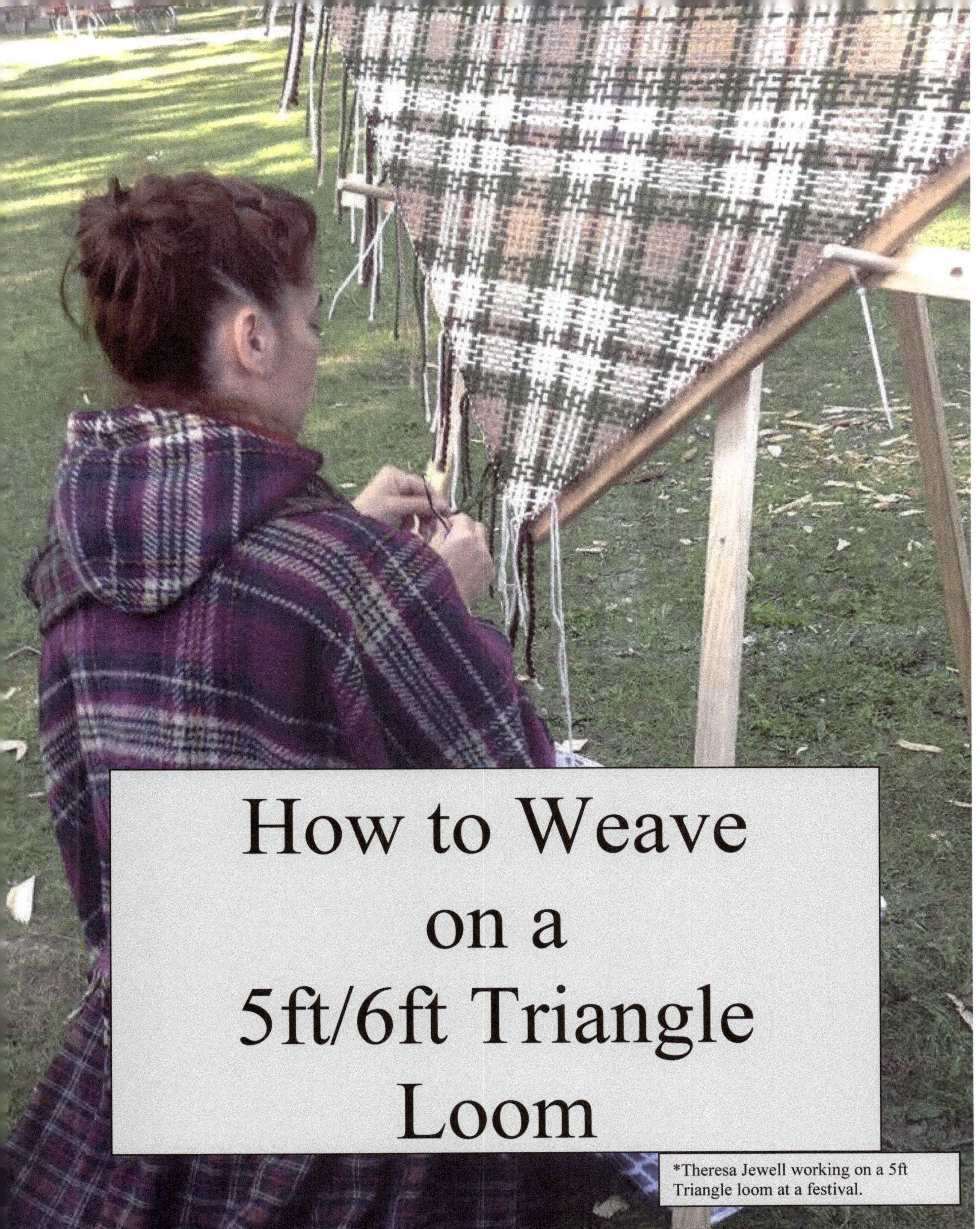

How to Weave on a 5ft/6ft Triangle Loom

*Theresa Jewell working on a 5ft Triangle loom at a festival.

Starting your Project

Before you start your project it's always a good idea to know how much yarn you need. If you're not sure, a good rule of thumb is to purchase more than you need of a particular color of yarn so you have the same dye lot. To complete the 5ft triangle loom, you need approximately 500 yards of yarn. This gives you a lot of wiggle room for mistakes, and a final border later.

The way we start and weave on the triangle looms differs a lot from other weavers online. Instead of the triangle pointing down, we point it up and work from the bottom up the loom.

Both Theresa and I are visual learners. Therefore, we will provide as many pictures as we can to help instruct you in starting your loom!

Let's get Started!

STEP 1: Starting in the lower left hand corner of the loom, place a slip knot over the corner nail.

STEP 2: Now take your working yarn 'for a walk' across the loom to the other corner. Here you are going to take your working yarn under the corner nail bringing it counterclockwise over the nail.

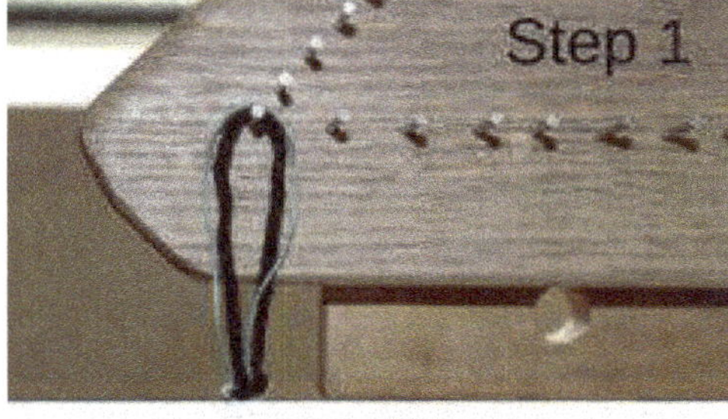

STEP 3: After you have the yarn on the right corner nail, walk your yarn back to the left where you started. Hook the working yarn on the nail above the nail with the slipknot on it. The yarn goes above the nail going counterclockwise over the nail to bring the working yarn down towards your feet. (Picture on next page)

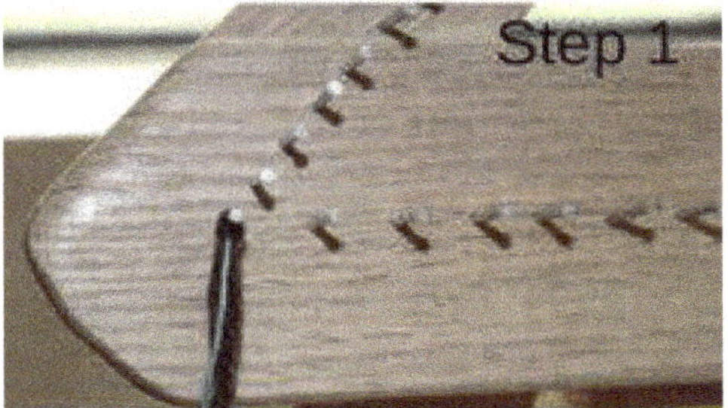

Your yarn should be hanging straight down off the second nail along the left side. We're going to start

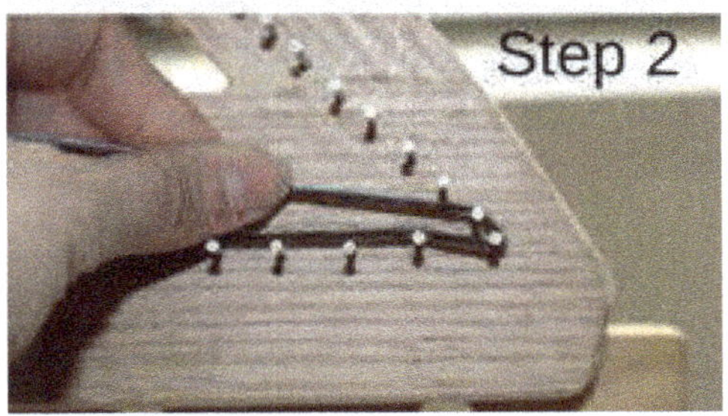

weaving now. You can either use your crochet hook, or you can use your fingers. Whichever is more comfortable for you.

STEP 4: Take your working yarn in your hand and bring it up around the first nail along the hypotenuse (longest side of triangle). Go under the first string and over the next string before you hook your yarn clockwise over the third nail on the left side.

> *I like to use my fingers for the first one and the crochet hook for the rest of the project.

At this point you should have 3 nails with yarn on them on the left side and one (or in my case two) on the right.

You have started your loom!

STEP 5: The yarn you just pulled clockwise over the third nail on the left is now 'taken for a walk' across the loom to the right side. Once there hook the yarn on the nail above the one with yarn on it. Hook the yarn clockwise on the nail and slide the woven bit into place on the left side.

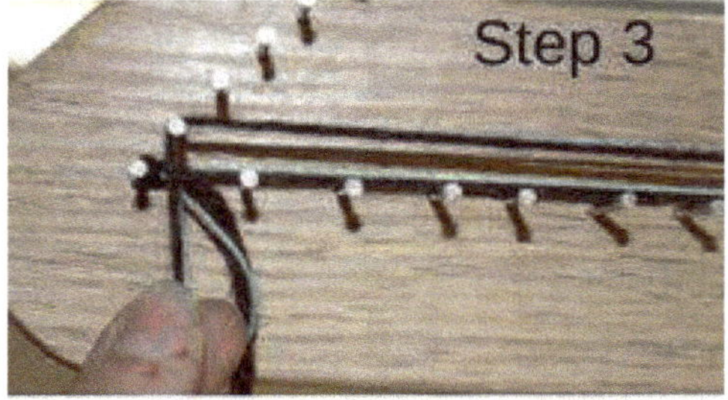

Now it's time to weave!

STEP 6: This time get your crochet hook and do the opposite of what you did the last time. In this case, going from the top using your crochet hook, go over, under, over. Hook your working yarn on the crochet hook and pull the yarn up through your work to the next free nail on the right side.

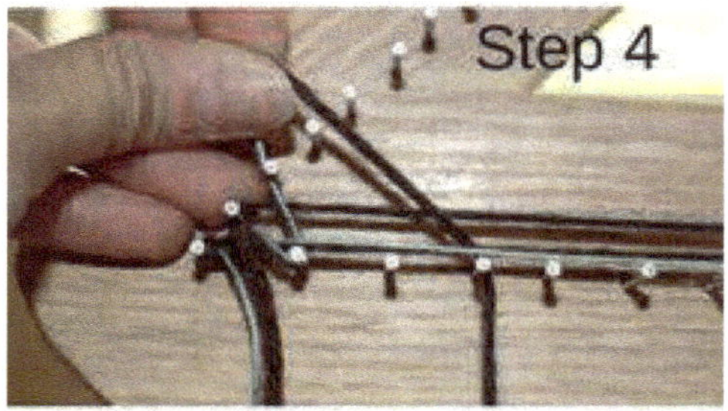

Repeat.

Take your yarn for a walk to the left. Hook the yarn onto the next available nail, slide weave into place and weaving from the top with your crochet hook bring the working yarn up to be placed onto the next nail.

Repeat process on the right side after taking your yarn for a walk.

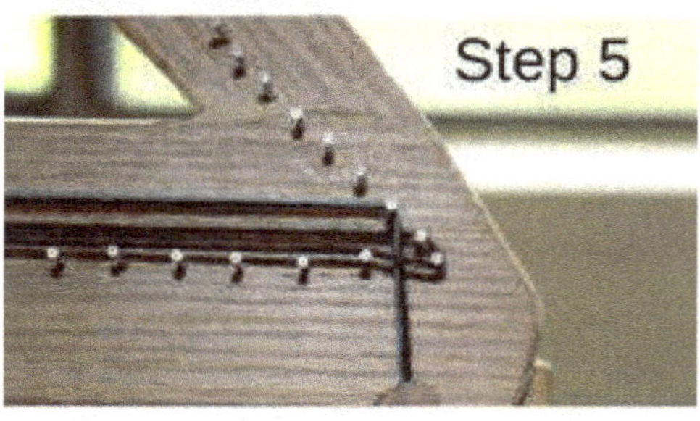

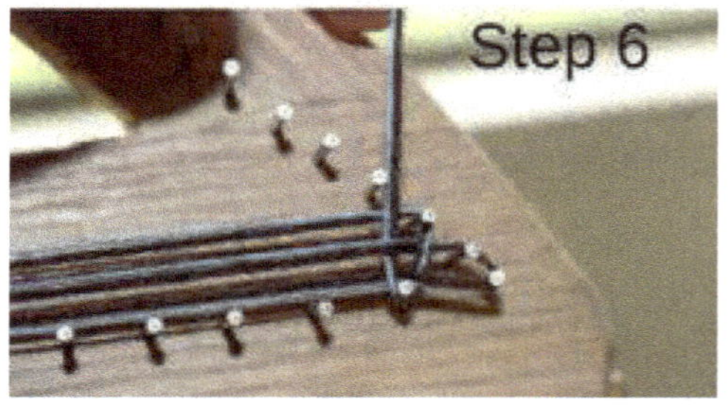

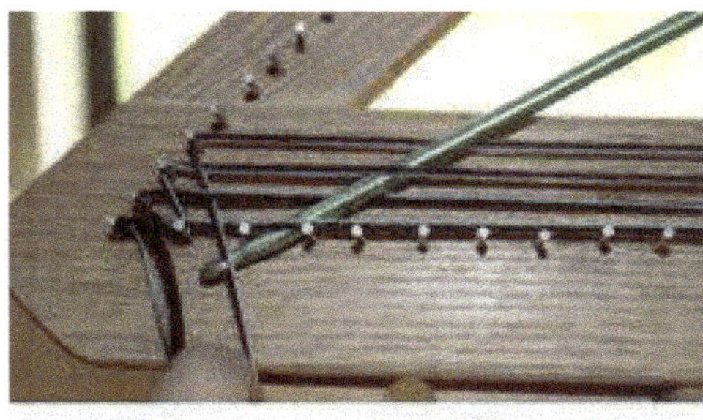

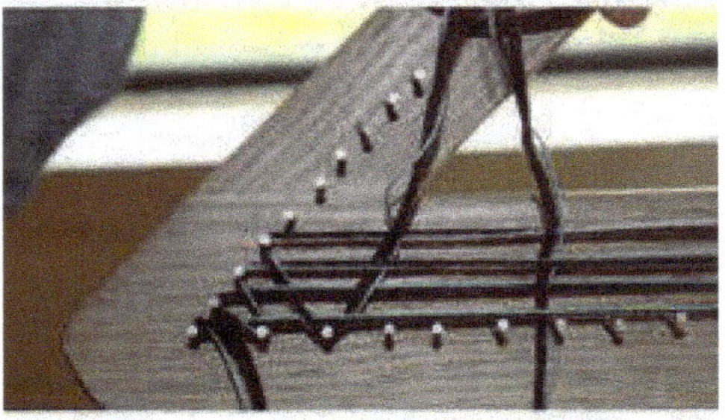

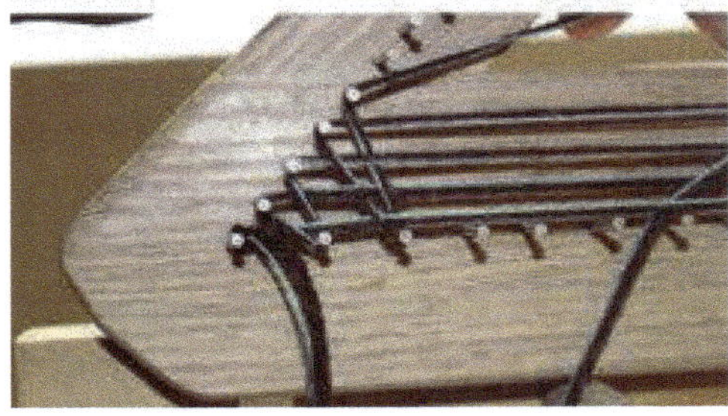

Some helpful tips:

•   Your yarn will always form a right angle on the side nails. If it doesn't, that means you forgot to take your yarn for a walk.

•   You will always be weaving two strings at one time.

•   You should always start weaving from the top by going over the first string on both the left and right sides of the loom.

•   Always make sure the yarn on the bottom nail is over and under the first string across so when you are ready to pull your work off the loom, it will not unravel.

•   At some point, it will become difficult to weave your crochet hook all the way through your work. This is when you start weaving a few strands at a time, starting from the bottom. This is hard to explain with words, turn the page to see picture by picture what I mean.

*I've included a quick reference section in the back of the book with all of Stone Mountains current looms and approximately how much yarn it takes to complete them.

Weaving when your crochet hook is too 'short'

       At some point, it will become difficult to weave your crochet hook all the way through your work. This is when you start weaving a few strands at a time, starting from the bottom. This is hard to explain with words, here are a few pictures and steps to help you.

Step 1: Weave part way through your weaving.

Step 2: Pull your working yarn up through the part you wove through.

Step 3: Keep weaving part of your work, always pulling your working yarn up through your work until you reach the top.

Step 4: Pull your working yarn all the way to the top of your work and hook on the appropriate nail, before taking your yarn for a walk and starting over on the opposite side.

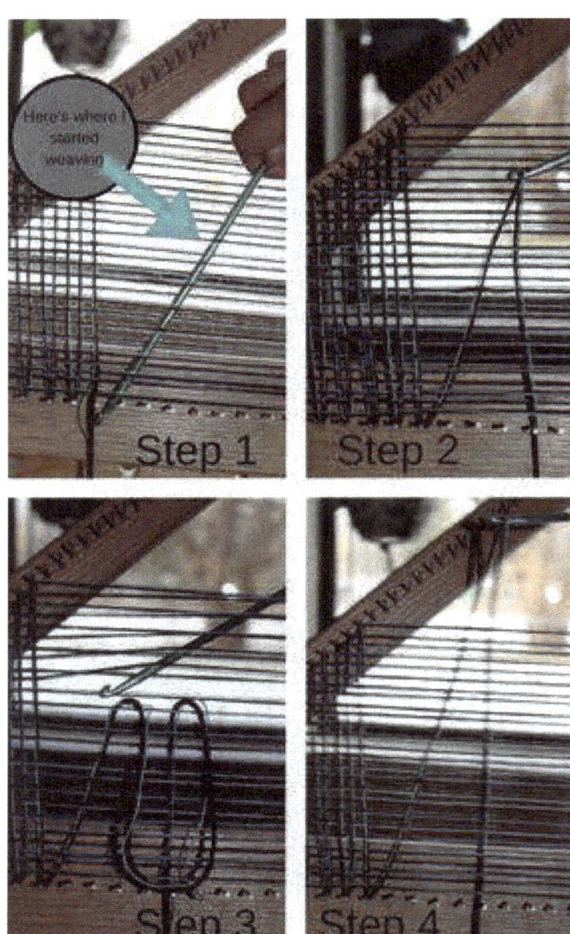

Fixing Common Mistakes

At some point in your weaving life you will find a mistake in your work. Don't worry, mistakes are easy to fix or you can leave the mistake. After all, this is a human made product. Mistakes can make your work unique.

Theresa and I make mistakes too, so don't worry. We can help you fix them! Here are the most common mistakes we come across and how to fix them.

Too Many Over's or Under's in a Row

A lot of the time you will be weaving and all of a sudden you'll realize you have three over's or under's in a row. And your pattern calls for over, under, over. You decide you want to fix it before you continue weaving.

Here's how:

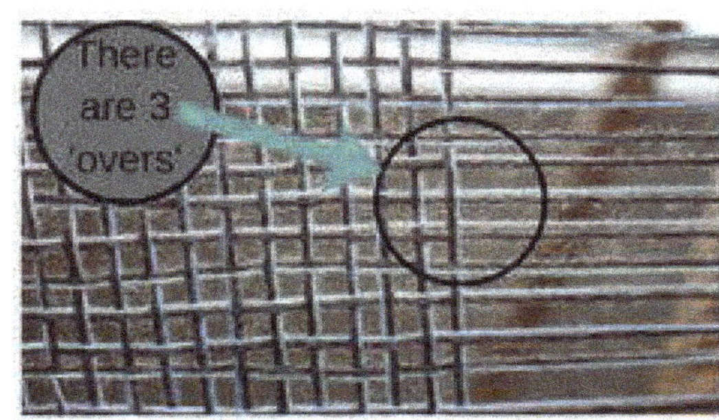

Step 1: Find your mistake.

Step 2: Find your working yarn and work backwards. Slip your working yarn off the last nail you placed it on. Walk to the other side of your loom and pull the yarn off the last nail on that side too.

Step 3: Now pull on your working yarn to unweave your work.

Step 4: Keep pulling out your weaving until you reach your mistake.

Step 5: Now it's time to reweave and 'fix' your mistake. Make sure you've fixed your mistake on both sides. *Remember, what you do to one side will happen to the other side.

Your mistake should be fixed, and now you're ready to continue weaving your project.

Your Yarn Breaks

Sometimes while you're weaving, especially if you are working with 1 ply yarn, your yarn with snap or break. You have several options before you so do not worry.

Your working yarn breaks while you are pulling it through the weaving. You can either pull out your work until you are on the left side of the loom where you can cut the broken piece off and treat it like you're changing colors. Tie the new end to the side, creating fringe and continue weaving.

A horizontal string breaks near the beginning of your work. This is scary and distressing, but we can fix it.

You can keep going as if the string is not broken and finish your work. When you go to fringe, or before you take your work off the loom, you can measure a new string to replace the broken one.

Before you pull the broken string out, here's a neat trick. You can take your new piece of yarn and tie one end to one of the broken ends. Now carefully pull the broken end with your new yarn attached through your weaving. Once you're at the end you can untie the strings, cut your broken string to fringe length and tie the new and old string together.

Now repeat with the other side.

By attaching the two strings together and pulling them through your work you eliminate the need to re-weave a new string in the old strings place. This goes quicker than if you were to pull the broken string out and using a tapestry needle re-weave the new string in its place.

Or

Tie off your working ends. And very carefully, cut your center strings 4 at a time. Tie off the strings as fringe as you go. Once you are all the way through your work, you can now pull it off the loom.

Here's where you can get creative. If you crochet or top stitch the two pieces you just created together, you can make a nice cowl. As the pattern in the Bonus Section shows you.

Changing Color Yarn

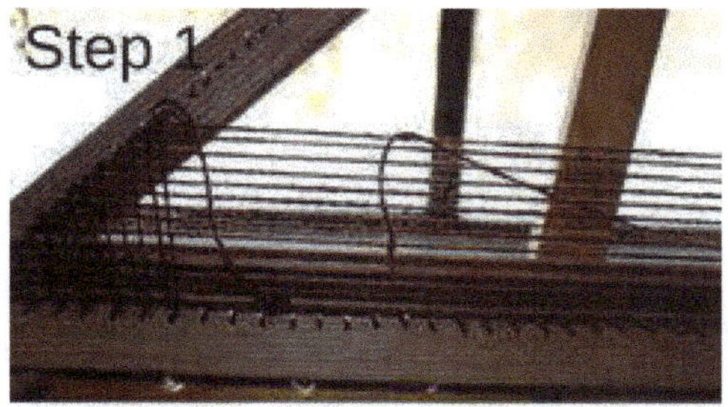

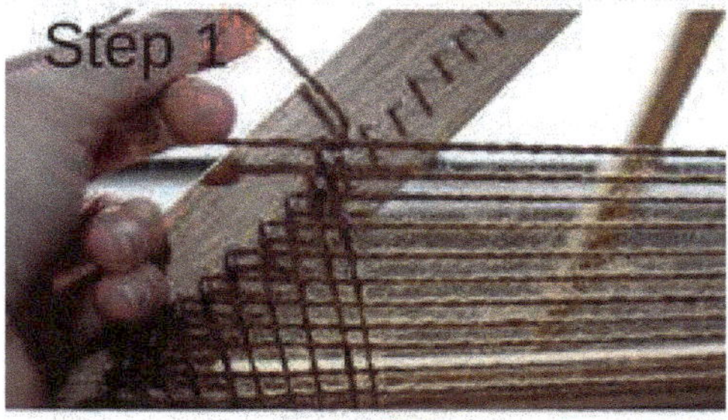

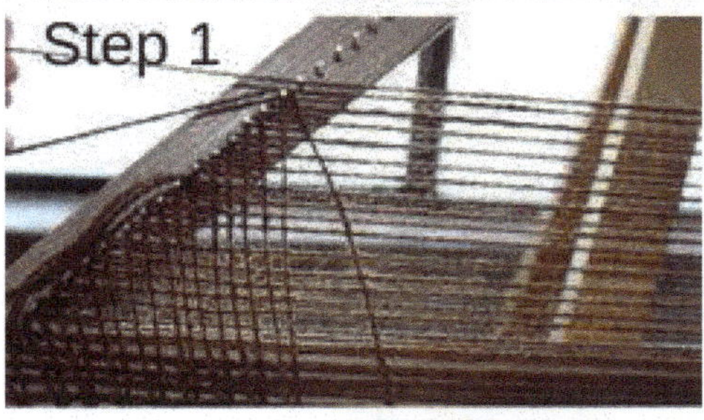

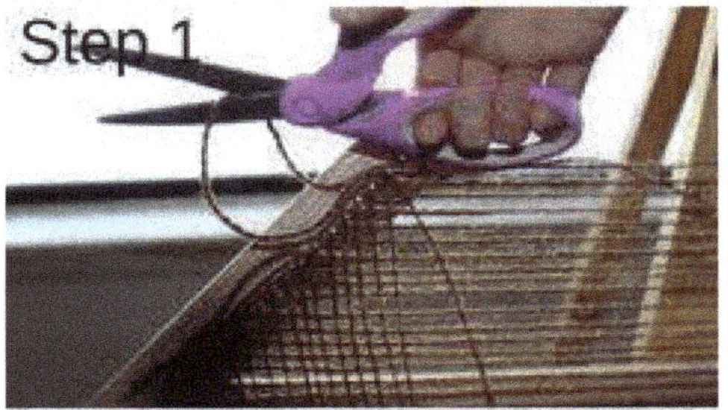

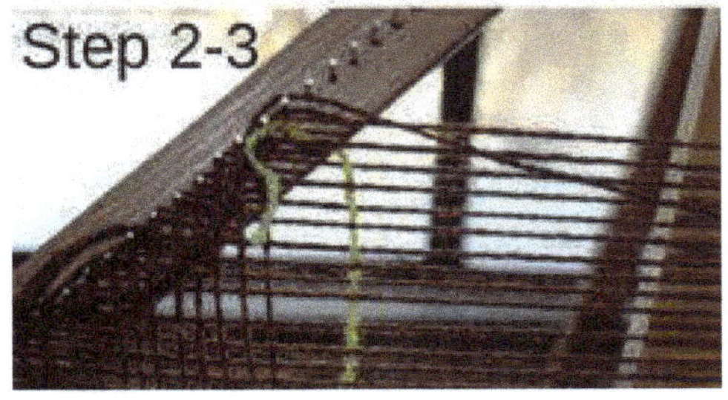

Now that you have the weaving basics down you can get adventurous and change color!

Is changing color hard?

*NO! It's not hard at all. It's more nerve wrecking because you're cutting your yarn which can be kind of scary. But we are going to walk you through it.

Step 1: Get to a place where you'd like to change color, or where the pattern changes color. Make sure you're working yarn is on the left side. The left side is where you will ALWAYS make your changes.

Get your scissors ready. Pull some slack up where your working yarn is over the top nail on the left side. If you're planning to leave fringe pull enough slack for the length of your fringe.

Cut your working yarn.

Step 2: Don't panic! You did not just ruin your work, I promise. We are now ready to change color. Pick up your new color yarn. Using your crochet hook, weave from the top down to the bottom of the loom, doing the opposite of what you just did on the left side of the loom. Draw the end of your new color up through your work.

Step 3: Pull enough of your new yarn through for the length of your fringe.

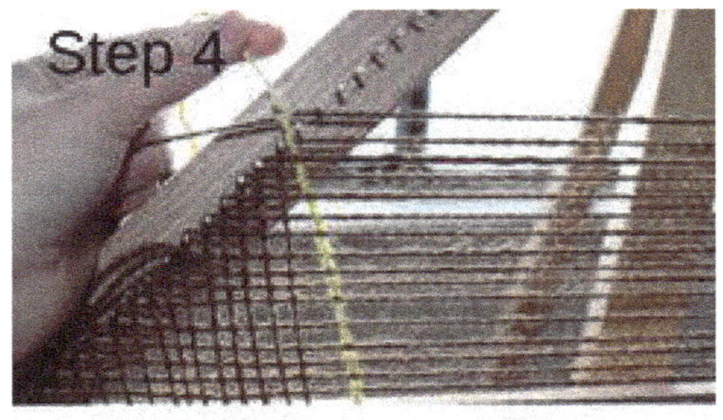

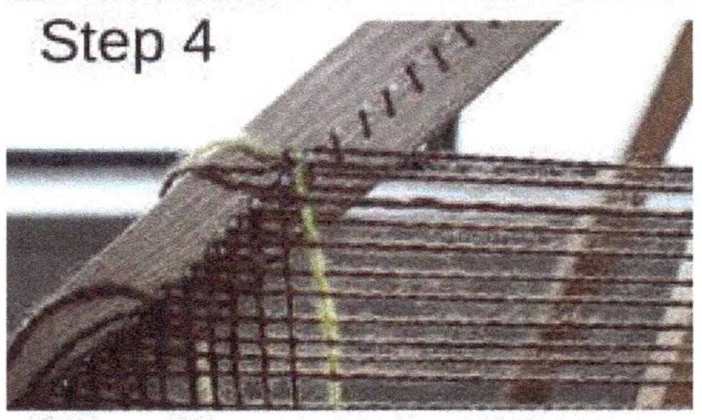

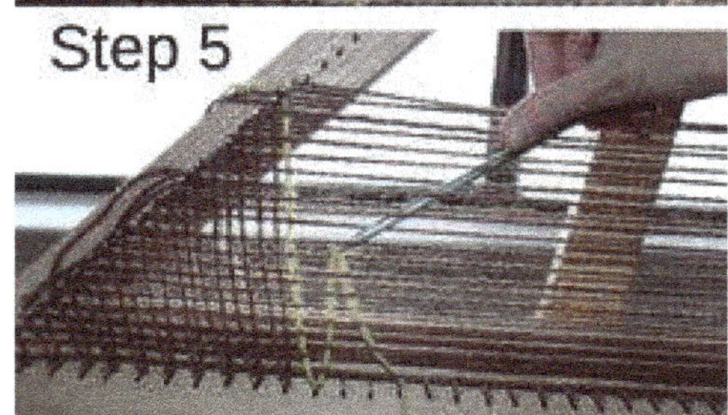

Step 4: Tie your new color with your old working yarn. A simple knot will do. Just make sure it is secure and not going to loosen or slide apart as you pull on your new yarn.

Step 5: Your new color is now attached. Now you once again take your crochet hook from the top of your work, weaving down to the bottom to pull your new working yarn up through the work. Take your new color for a walk after hooking it on the next available nail and continue weaving.

You've successfully changed colors! You can change colors as often as you'd like throughout your work. Or you can follow our patterns for two or more colors.

Happy weaving!

Finishing your Project

You've just finished weaving the entire triangle, now what? It's time to finish your project and get it off the loom where you can add embellishments like a crocheted border, if you'd like.

We recommend when you get to the center nail of your hypotenuse, you stop weaving for a minute. Yes, you have one more strand to weave up through your work. You can weave two strands up through your work like you have been this whole time or you can, without weaving, bring your working yarn up to the top of your loom.

Leaving enough room for fringe, cut your working yarn.

Now you can weave the final strand up through your work.

> *Weaving the last string can be hard to do depending on your tension. That's why we like to cut our last piece of yarn before we weave it up through the center. Bringing one string up is a lot easier to do than two.

When you get to the top, it's time to tie off. You want to tie your last string to the work so it does not unweave.

You also want to tie off your slip knot. I find slipping my slip knot off the first nail before I tie it off easier than trying to pull it off after I've tied it off. You can tie off either before or after you take the slip knot off, it's up to you.

Fringe Border

Now that everything is tied off, it's time to add fringe! *If you don't want to add fringe you can skip ahead to taking your work of your loom.

Both Theresa and I use a knitting needle gauge card to help us measure our fringe (Shown left). We simply wrap our yarn around the gauge and cut it, making uniform pieces of yarn.

Using either your crochet hook or a latch hook attach your fringe to your work. We recommend you attach fringe in between every other nail. Pull one side of the fringe through your work and tie with a simple knot.

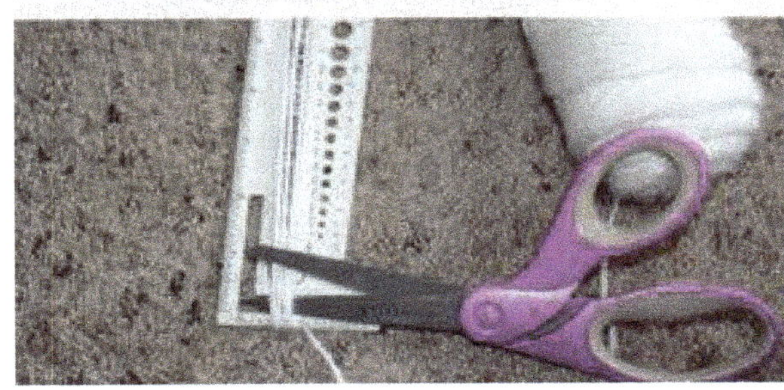

> *I find a latch hook is a lot easier

If you changed color on your work, we recommend you tie the color change ends with the fringe you're adding.

Once you have all the fringe on, you can now take your work

off the loom. Just lift your woven edges up and off the nails. Be careful not to snag your yarn as you pull your work off evenly.

You're almost done!

Now that your work is off the loom, take a look at the hypotenuse side (the side without fringe). It doesn't look very finished. We recommend a single crochet chain to finish off the edge to make your work look beautiful!

Now you are finished. You made something beautiful and you should be proud!

Crochet Border

You've finished your work and have decided to go with a crochet border instead of fringe. Tie off your working ends and carefully pull your work off the loom.

Theresa prefers to crochet borders after her work is off the loom. However, there are others who prefer to crochet their work as they take it off the loom. Do whichever is more comfortable for you.

Once your work is off the loom, find an appropriate size crochet hook and the yarn you'd like to use to make your border. There are so many different beautiful crochet borders available, we recommend you find one you like and follow the crochet instructions available.

Other Borders

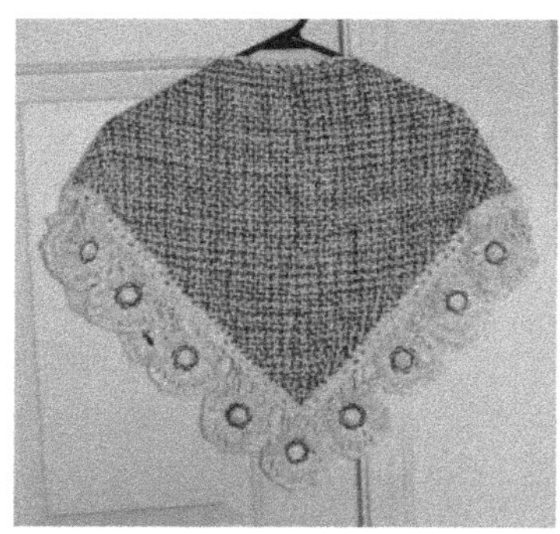

Always remember the sky is the limit. There are so many other ways to finish your products, do not feel limited by the two options we have provided.

Stoney Meadows Alpacas and Stone Mountain Looms have a new loom available called a flower loom. This loom creates adorable flowers that can be used in your work.

Unfortunately, I did not have access to a 5ft triangle loom to create something on in, but this shawl was created on a 3ft triangle loom with a crochet flower border. Always remember the sky is the limit, so get creative and have fun!

Reading Our Patterns

To make our patterns as accessible as they can be, we have provided two different styles. The first is written out like a knitting or crochet pattern and the second is a visual chart.

The written pattern starts on the first nail along the hypotenuse. This means your slip knot. The second nail will be the nail next to your slip knot on the left side. Remember you are weaving two sides at once to create a mirror image across the center nail which if you purchased a triangle loom from Stoney Meadow Alpacas and Stone Mountain Looms, will be marked. The pattern is worked from the left and will end on the center nail or nail 61 in this case.

*There are 122 nails along the hypotenuse of the 5ft triangle. Since you are weaving two strands at a time, filling in two sides at once, the pattern will only cover 61 nails. Trust me, your project will be complete after you follow the pattern for 61 nails.

We use all the same abbreviations as knitting or crochet patterns.

For example:
Nail 1-3 (3 nails): Blue
Nail 4-8 (5 nails): Red
Nail 9-10 (2 nails): Green
Nail 11-15 (5 nails): Red
Nail 16-20 (5 nails): Blue

The visual chart shows all the nails from the first to the center mark on your loom. Remember, everything you do to your nails on the left will be repeated on the right.
*This is an example, not a complete pattern!

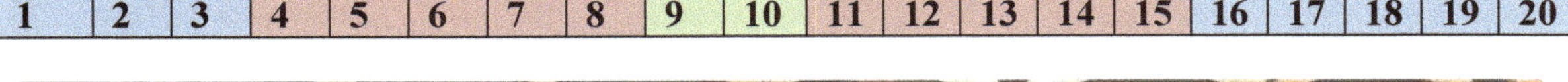

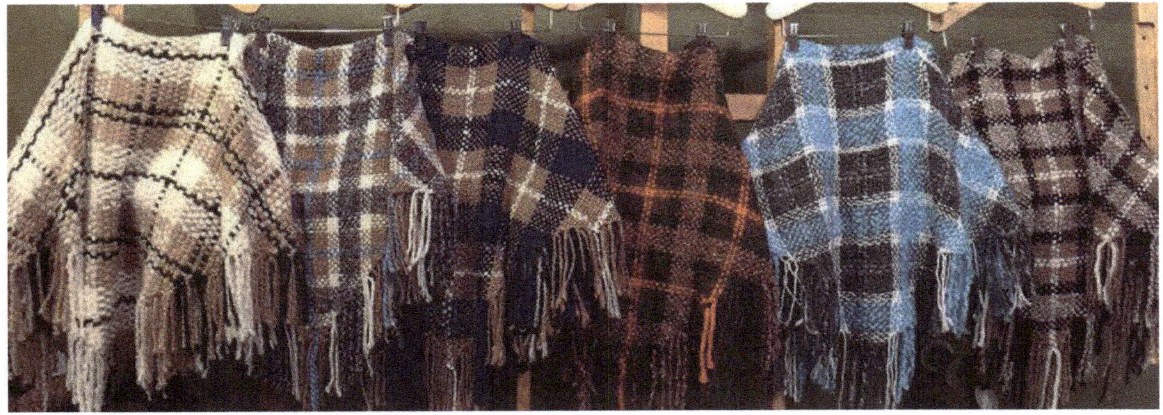

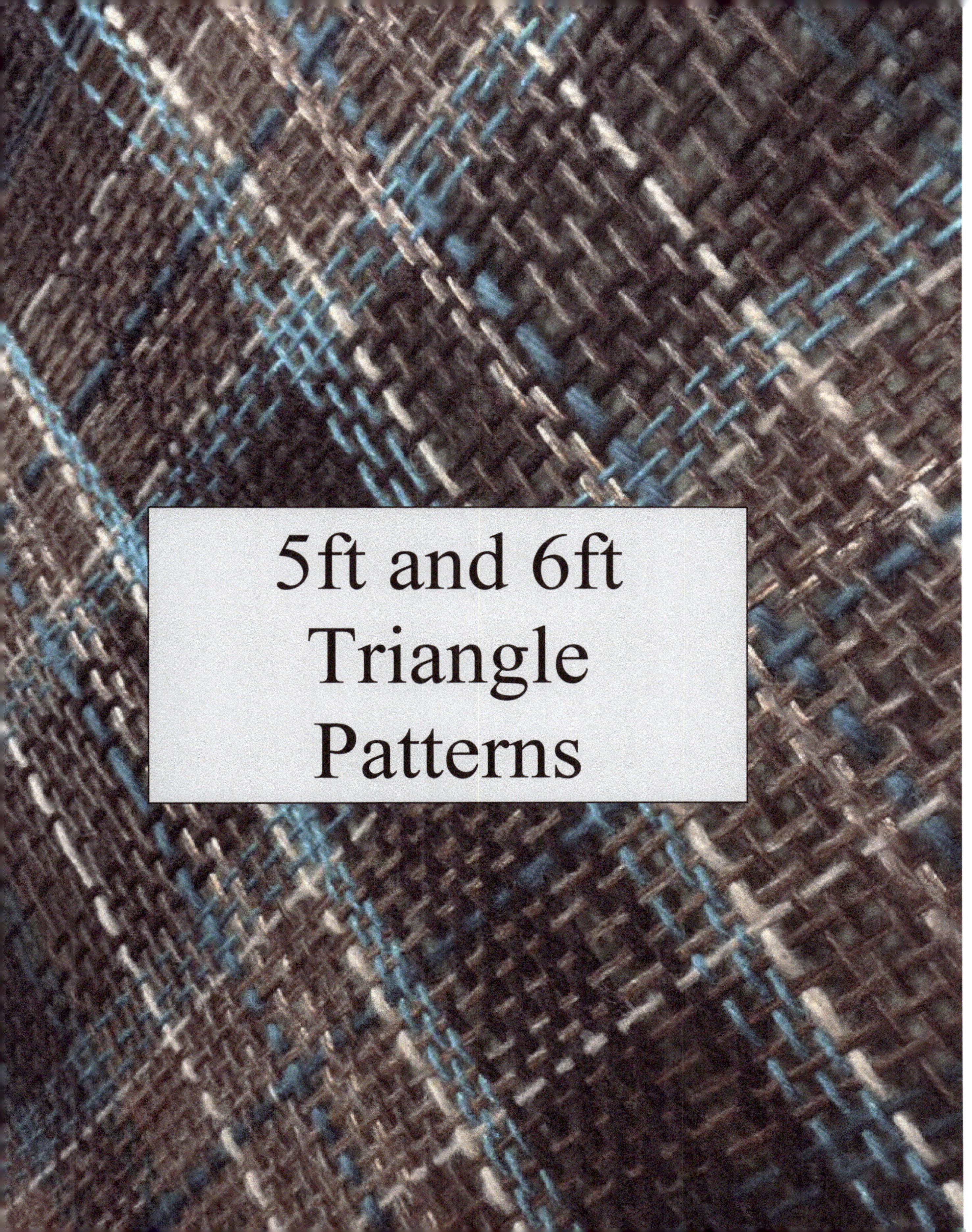

5ft and 6ft
Triangle
Patterns

One Color Projects

Difficulty: *

When using one color, weaving goes quick and easy. To add variation to the one color we recommend picking a variegated yarn. You'll be surprised how the yarn creates interesting colors throughout the work.

Pattern 1
5ft Triangle

Nail 1-61(61 nails): Blue
Tie off slip knot and last woven strand.
Add any last minute embellishments (Fringe) and then pull off your loom.

1	2	3	4	5	6	7	8	9	10	11	12	13	14	15	16	17	18	19	20
21	22	23	24	25	26	27	28	29	30	31	32	33	34	35	36	37	38	39	40
41	42	43	44	45	46	47	48	49	50	51	52	53	54	55	56	57	58	59	60
61																			

6ft triangle conversion

Nail 1-73 (73 nails): Blue
Tie off slip knot and last woven strand.
Add any last minute embellishments (Fringe) and then pull of your loom.

1	2	3	4	5	6	7	8	9	10	11	12	13	14	15	16	17	18	19	20
21	22	23	24	25	26	27	28	29	30	31	32	33	34	35	36	37	38	39	40
41	42	43	44	45	46	47	48	49	50	51	52	53	54	55	56	57	58	59	60
61	62	63	64	65	66	67	68	69	70	71	72	73							

Two Strand Shawl with Crochet Boarder

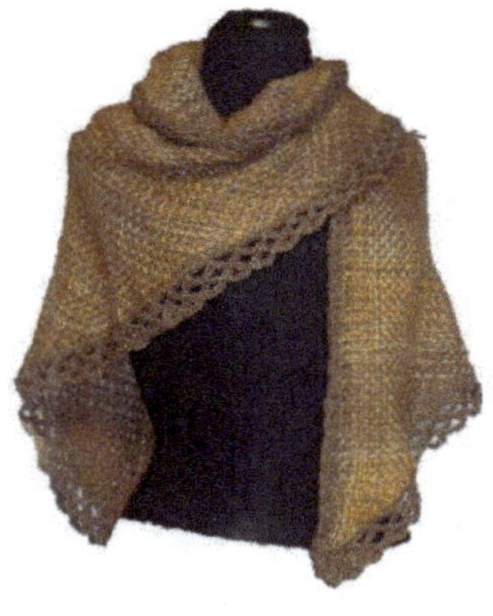

This beautiful shawl is made by weaving two strands of yarn together at once. The first strand is a solid fawn alpaca yarn, the other is a pumpkin gradient. To finish it off, Theresa added a crocheted boarder.

There are no color changes for this pattern, just start weaving with the two colors of yarn until the project is complete.

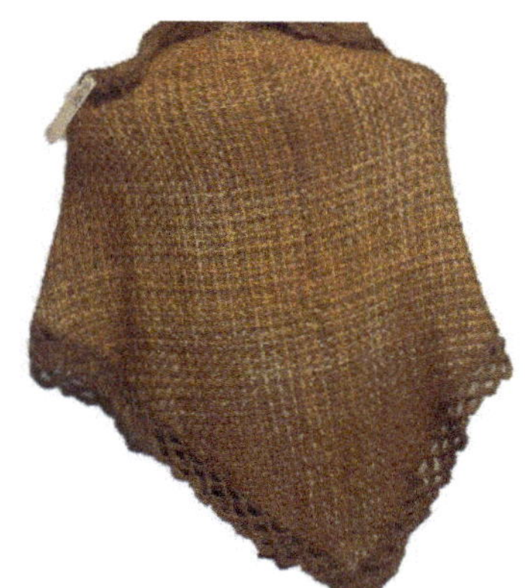

Difficulty: *

Pattern 2
5ft Triangle

Nail 1-61 (61 nails): Tan
Tie off slip knot and last woven strand.
Add any last minute embellishments (Fringe) and then pull off your loom.

1	2	3	4	5	6	7	8	9	10	11	12	13	14	15	16	17	18	19	20
21	22	23	24	25	26	27	28	29	30	31	32	33	34	35	36	37	38	39	40
41	42	43	44	45	46	47	48	49	50	51	52	53	54	55	56	57	58	59	60
61																			

6ft triangle conversion

Nail 1-73 (73 nails): Tan
Tie off slip knot and last woven strand.
Add any last minute embellishments (Fringe) and then pull of your loom.

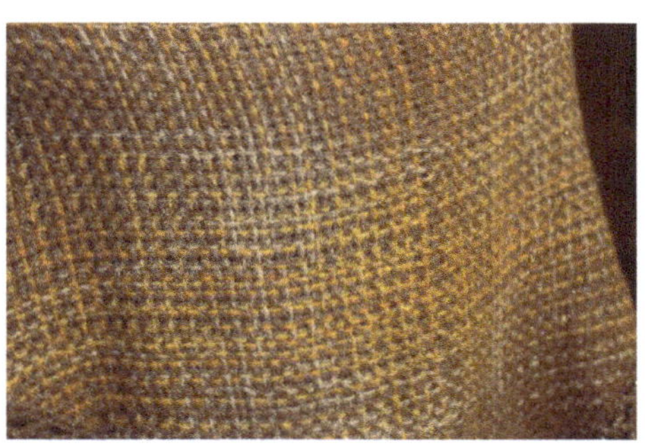

1	2	3	4	5	6	7	8	9	10	11	12	13	14	15	16	17	18	19	20
21	22	23	24	25	26	27	28	29	30	31	32	33	34	35	36	37	38	39	40
41	42	43	44	45	46	47	48	49	50	51	52	53	54	55	56	57	58	59	60
61	62	63	64	65	66	67	68	69	70	71	72	73							

Two Color Projects

Difficulty: **

**Pattern 3 – Berry Patch
5ft Triangle**

<u>Approximate Yardage:</u>

Purple: 170 yards
Brown: 72 yards

Nail 1-5 (5 nails): Brown
Nail 6 (1 nail): Purple
Nail 7-9 (2 nails): Brown
Nail 9 (1 nail): Purple
Nail 10-15 (6 nails): Brown
Nail 16 (1 nail): Purple
Nail 17-22 (6 nails): Brown
Nail 23 (1 nail): Purple
Nail 24-29 (6 nails): Brown

Repeat Nails 6-30 *Once*

Nail 55-60 (6 nails): Brown
Nail 61 (1 nail): Purple

Tie off slip knot and last woven strand.
Add any last minute embellishments (Fringe) and then pull off your loom.

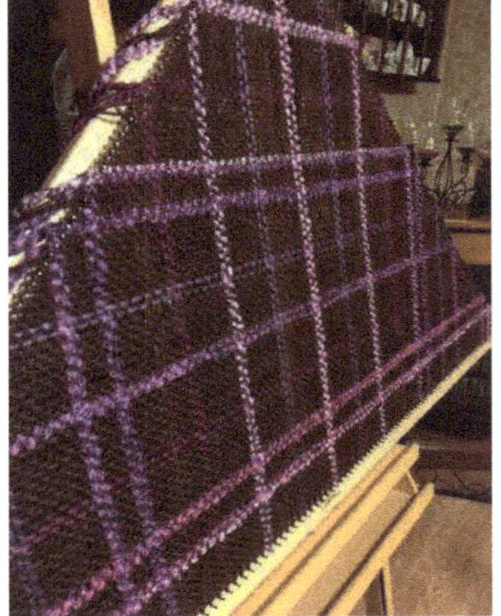

1	2	3	4	5	6	7	8	9	10	11	12	13	14	15	16	17	18	19	20
21	22	23	24	25	26	27	28	29	30	31	32	33	34	35	36	37	38	39	40
41	42	43	44	45	46	47	48	49	50	51	52	53	54	55	56	57	58	59	60
61																			

6ft Triangle Conversion

Approximate Yardage:

Purple: 192 yards
Brown: 81 yards

Nail 1-3 (3 nails): Brown
Nail 4 (1 nail): Purple
Nail 5-10 (6 nails): Brown
Nail 11 (1 nail): Purple
Nail 12-13 (2 nails): Brown
Nail 14 (1 nail): Purple
Nail 15-20 (6 nails): Brown
Nail 21 (1 nail): Purple
Nail 22-27 (6 nails): Brown
Nail 28 (1 nail): Purple
Nail 29-34 (6 nails): Brown
Nail 35 (1 nail): Purple
Nail 36-41 (6 nails): Brown

Repeat Nail 11-42 *Once*

Tie off slip knot and last woven strand.
Add any last minute embellishments
(Fringe) and then pull off your loom.

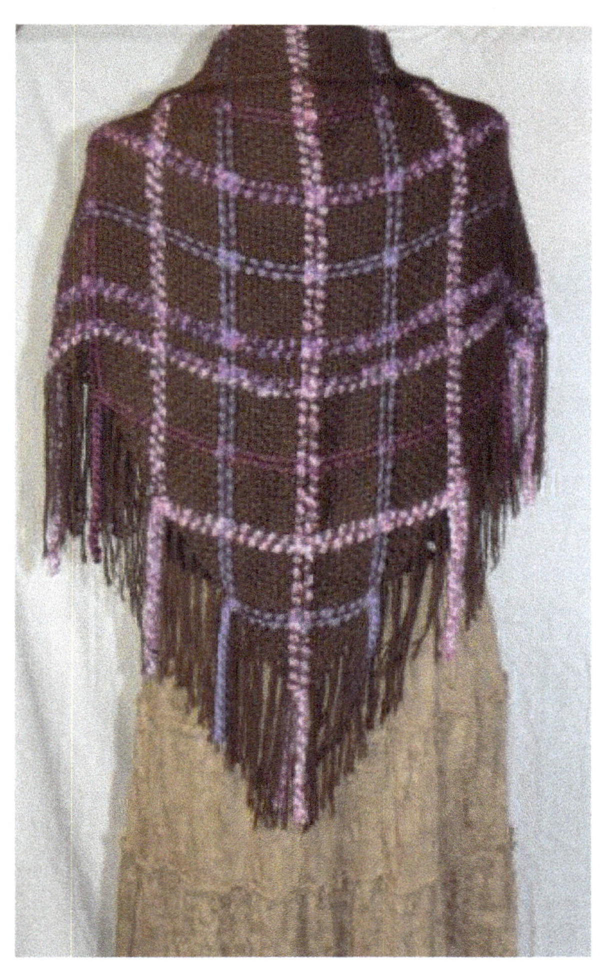

1	2	3	4	5	6	7	8	9	10	11	12	13	14	15	16	17	18	19	20
21	22	23	24	25	26	27	28	29	30	31	32	33	34	35	36	37	38	39	40
41	42	43	44	45	46	47	48	49	50	51	52	53	54	55	56	57	58	59	60
61	62	63	64	65	66	67	68	69	70	71	72	73							

Difficulty: **

**Pattern 4 – Traditional Checkers
5ft Triangle**

<u>Approximate Yardage:</u>

White: 152 yards
Black: 90 yards

Nail 1-3 (3 nails): White
Nail 4-6 (3 nails): Black
Nail 7-11 (5 nails): White

Repeat Nail 4-11 *six times*

Nail 60-61: Black

Tie off slip knot and last woven strand.
Add any last minute embellishments
(Fringe) and then pull off your loom.

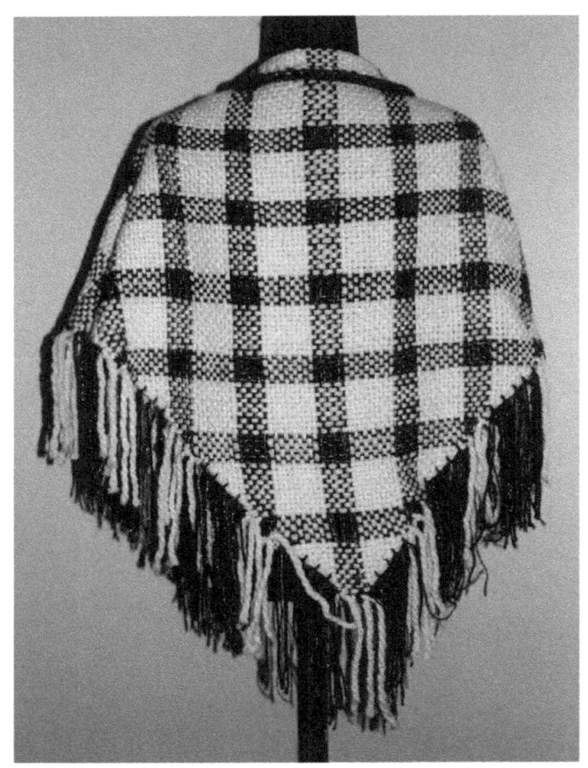

1	2	3	4	5	6	7	8	9	10	11	12	13	14	15	16	17	18	19	20
21	22	23	24	25	26	27	28	29	30	31	32	33	34	35	36	37	38	39	40
41	42	43	44	45	46	47	48	49	50	51	52	53	54	55	56	57	58	59	60
61																			

6ft Triangle Conversion

<u>Approximate Yardage:</u>

White: 171 yards
Black: 102 yards

Nail 1-2 (2 nails): Black
Nail 3-7 (5 nails): White
Nail 8-10 (3 nails): Black

Repeat Nail 3-10 *seven times*

Nail 67-71 (5 nails): White
Nail 72-73 (2 nails): Black

Tie off slip knot and last woven strand.
Add any last minute embellishments (Fringe) and then pull off your loom.

1	2	3	4	5	6	7	8	9	10	11	12	13	14	15	16	17	18	19	20
21	22	23	24	25	26	27	28	29	30	31	32	33	34	35	36	37	38	39	40
41	42	43	44	45	46	47	48	49	50	51	52	53	54	55	56	57	58	59	60
61	62	63	64	65	66	67	68	69	70	71	72	73							

Difficulty: **

**Pattern 5 – Murky Waters
5ft Triangle**

<u>Approximate Yardage:</u>

Blue: 76 yards
Brown: 166 yards

Nail 1-4 (4 nails): Blue
Nail 5-13 (9 nails): Brown
Nail 14-17 (4 nails): Blue
Nail 18-25 (8 nails): Brown
Nail 26-28 (3 nails): Blue
Nail 29-35 (7 nails): Brown
Nail 36-38 (3 nails): Blue
Nail 39-44 (6 nails): Brown
Nail 45-46 (2 nails): Blue
Nail 47-51 (5 nails): Brown
Nail 52-53 (2 nails): Blue
Nail 54-57 (4 nails): Brown
Nail 58 (1 nails): Blue
Nail 59-60 (3 nails): Brown

Tie off slip knot and last woven strand.
Add any last minute embellishments (Fringe) and then pull off your loom.

1	2	3	4	5	6	7	8	9	10	11	12	13	14	15	16	17	18	19	20
21	22	23	24	25	26	27	28	29	30	31	32	33	34	35	36	37	38	39	40
41	42	43	44	45	46	47	48	49	50	51	52	53	54	55	56	57	58	59	60
61																			

6ft Triangle Conversion

Approximate Yardage:

Blue: 86 yards
Brown: 241 yards

Nail 1-12 (12 nails): Brown
Nail 13-16 (4 nails): Blue
Nail 17-25 (9 nails): Brown
Nail 26-29 (4 nails): Blue
Nail 30-37 (8 nails): Brown
Nail 38-40 (3 nails): Blue
Nail 41-47 (7 nails): Brown
Nail 48-50 (3 nails): Blue
Nail 51-56 (6 nails): Brown
Nail 57-58 (2 nails): Blue
Nail 59-63 (5 nails): Brown
Nail 64-65 (2 nails): Blue
Nail 66-69 (4 nails): Brown
Nail 70 (1 nail): Blue
Nail 71-73 (3 nails): Brown

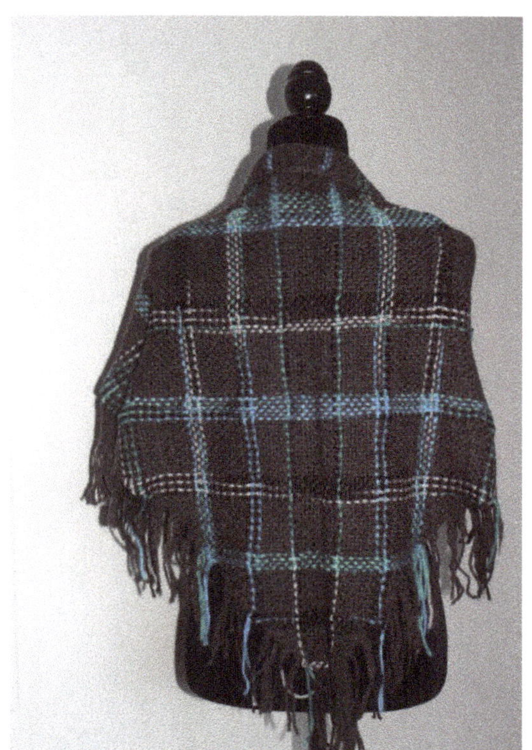

Tie off slip knot and last woven strand.
Add any last minute embellishments (Fringe) and then pull off your loom.

1	2	3	4	5	6	7	8	9	10	11	12	13	14	15	16	17	18	19	20
21	22	23	24	25	26	27	28	29	30	31	32	33	34	35	36	37	38	39	40
41	42	43	44	45	46	47	48	49	50	51	52	53	54	55	56	57	58	59	60
61	62	63	64	65	66	67	68	69	70	71	72	73							

NEW

Difficulty: **

**Pattern 5.5– Well Played Plaid
5ft Triangle**

<u>Approximate Yardage:</u>

Gray: 146 yards
Red: 96 yards

Nail 1-3 (3 nails): Gray
Nail 4-6 (3 nails): Red
Nail 7 (1 nail): Gray
Nail 8-10 (3 nails): Red
Nail 11-15 (5 nails): Gray
Nail 16 (1 nail): Red
Nail 17-21 (5 nails): Gray

Repeat Nails 4-21 *two times*

Nail 58-60 (3 nails): Red
Nail 61 (1 nail): Gray

Tie off slip knot and last woven strand.
Add any last minute embellishments (Fringe) and then pull off your loom

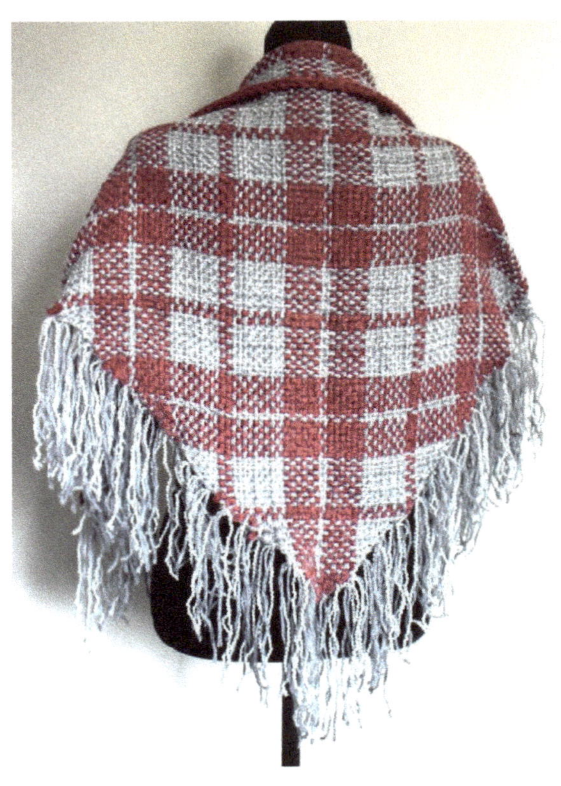

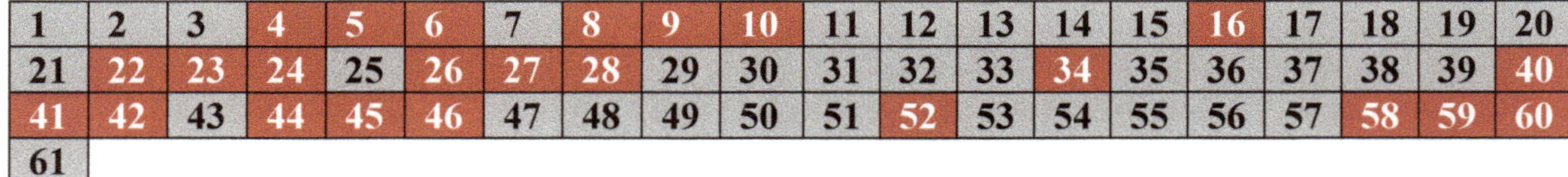

1	2	3	4	5	6	7	8	9	10	11	12	13	14	15	16	17	18	19	20
21	22	23	24	25	26	27	28	29	30	31	32	33	34	35	36	37	38	39	40
41	42	43	44	45	46	47	48	49	50	51	52	53	54	55	56	57	58	59	60
61																			

6ft Triangle Conversion

<u>Approximate Yardage</u>:

Gray: 196 yards
Red: 131 yards

Nail 1-4 (4 nails): Red
Nail 5-9 (5 nails): Gray
Nail 10 (1 nail): Red
Nail 11-15 (5 nails): Gray
Nail 16-18 (3 nails): Red
Nail 19 (1 nails): Gray
Nail 20-22 (3 nails): Red

Repeat Nails 5-22 *two times*

Nail 59-63 (5 nails): Gray
Nail 64 (1 nail): Red
Nail 65-69 (5 nails): Gray
Nail 70-72 (3 nails): Red
Nail 73 (1 nail): Gray

Tie off slip knot and last woven strand.
Add any last minute embellishments (Fringe) and then pull off your loom

1	2	3	4	5	6	7	8	9	10	11	12	13	14	15	16	17	18	19	20
21	22	23	24	25	26	27	28	29	30	31	32	33	34	35	36	37	38	39	40
41	42	43	44	45	46	47	48	49	50	51	52	53	54	55	56	57	58	59	60
61	62	63	64	65	66	67	68	69	70	71	72	73							

Three Color Projects

Difficulty: **

**Pattern 6- Checkerboard
5ft Triangle**

Approximate Yardage:

Light Brown: 84 yards
Dark Brown: 128 yards
White: 32 yards

Nail 1-3 (3 nails): Light Brown
Nail 4 (1 nail): White
Nail 5-12 (8 nails): Dark Brown
Nail 13 (1 nail): White
Nail 14-18 (5 nails): Light Brown

Repeat Nails 4-13 *three times*

Nail 59-61: Light Brown

Tie off slip knot and last woven strand.
Add any last minute embellishments (Fringe) and then pull off your loom

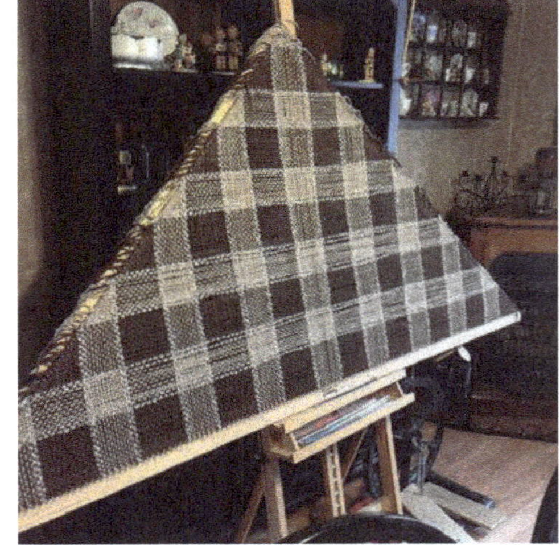

1	2	3	4	5	6	7	8	9	10	11	12	13	14	15	16	17	18	19	20
21	22	23	24	25	26	27	28	29	30	31	32	33	34	35	36	37	38	39	40
41	42	43	44	45	46	47	48	49	50	51	52	53	54	55	56	57	58	59	60
61																			

6ft Triangle Conversion

<u>Approximate Yardage</u>:

Light Brown: 102 yards
Dark Brown: 185 yards
White: 41 yards

Nail 1-9 (9 nails): Dark Brown
Nail 10 (1 nail): White
Nail 11-15 (5 nails): Light Brown
Nail 16 (1 nail): White

Repeat Nail 2-16 *three times*

Nail 62-69 (9 nails): Dark Brown
Nail 70 (1 nail): White
Nail 71-73 (3 nails): Light Brown

Tie off slip knot and last woven strand.
Add any last minute embellishments (Fringe) and then pull off your loom.

1	2	3	4	5	6	7	8	9	10	11	12	13	14	15	16	17	18	19	20
21	22	23	24	25	26	27	28	29	30	31	32	33	34	35	36	37	38	39	40
41	42	43	44	45	46	47	48	49	50	51	52	53	54	55	56	57	58	59	60
61	62	63	64	65	66	67	68	69	70	71	72	73							

Difficulty: **

Pattern 7– Autumn Sky
5ft Triangle

<u>Approximate Yardage:</u>

White: 188 yards
Orange: 36 yards
Red: 16 yards

Nail 1-3 (3 nails): White
Nail 4 (1 nail): Orange
Nail 5 (1 nail): White
Nail 6 (1 nail): Orange
Nail 7-11 (5 nails): White
Nail 12 (1 nail): Red
Nail 13-17 (5 nails): White

Repeat Nails 4-17 ***three times***

Nail 60 (1 nail): Orange
Nail 61 (1 nail): White

Tie off slip knot and last woven strand.
Add any last minute embellishments (Fringe) and then pull off your loom.

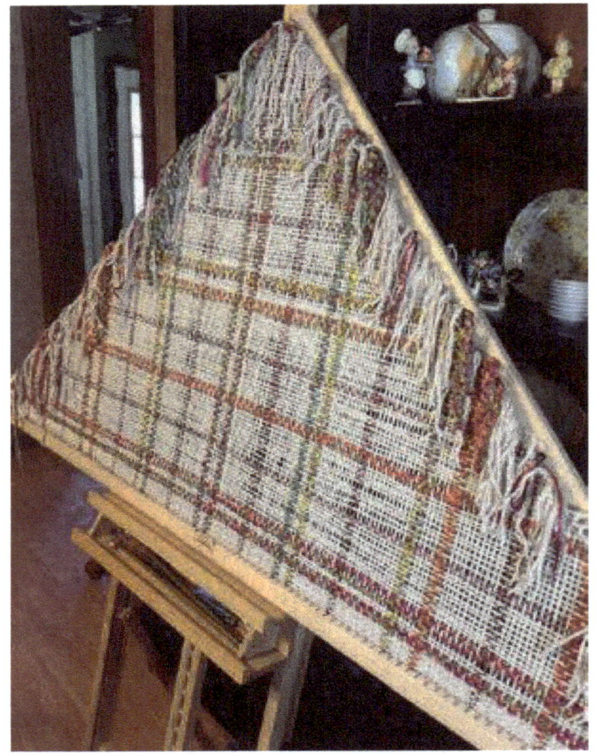

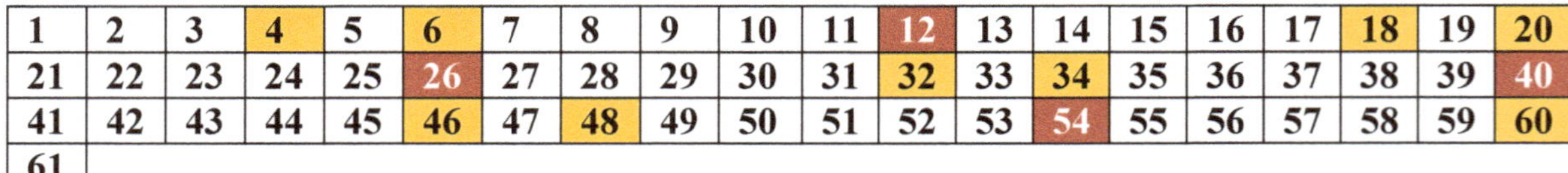

1	2	3	4	5	6	7	8	9	10	11	12	13	14	15	16	17	18	19	20
21	22	23	24	25	26	27	28	29	30	31	32	33	34	35	36	37	38	39	40
41	42	43	44	45	46	47	48	49	50	51	52	53	54	55	56	57	58	59	60
61																			

6ft Triangle Conversion

Approximate Yardage:

White: 259 yards
Orange: 45 yards
Red: 23 yards

Nail 1-3 (3 nails): White
Nail 4 (1 nail): Orange
Nail 5-9 (5 nail): White
Nail 10 (1 nail): Red
Nail 11-15 (5 nails): White
Nail 16 (1 nail): Orange

Repeat Nails 3-16 *four times*

Tie off slip knot and last woven strand.
Add any last minute embellishments (Fringe) and then pull off your loom.

1	2	3	4	5	6	7	8	9	10	11	12	13	14	15	16	17	18	19	20
21	22	23	24	25	26	27	28	29	30	31	32	33	34	35	36	37	38	39	40
41	42	43	44	45	46	47	48	49	50	51	52	53	54	55	56	57	58	59	60
61	62	63	64	65	66	67	68	69	70	71	72	73							

Difficulty: **

**Pattern 8– Well Played Plaid
5ft Triangle**

<u>Approximate Yardage:</u>

White: 96 yards
Green: 32 yards
Tan: 114 yards

Nail 1-6 (6 nails): Tan
Nail 7-10 (4 nails): White
Nail 11 (1 nail): Green
Nail 12-15 (4 nails): White
Nail 16-19 (4 nails): Tan
Nail 20 (1 nail): Green
Nail 21 (1 nail): Tan
Nail 22 (1 nail: Green
Nail 23-26 (4 nails): Tan

*Repeat Nail 7-26 *once*

Nail 47-50 (4 nails): White
Nail 51 (1 nail): Green
Nail 52-55 (4 nails): White
Nail 56-59 (4 nails): Tan
Nail 60 (1 nail): Green
Nail 61 (1 nail): Tan

Tie off slip knot and last woven strand.
Add any last minute embellishments (Fringe) and then pull off your loom.

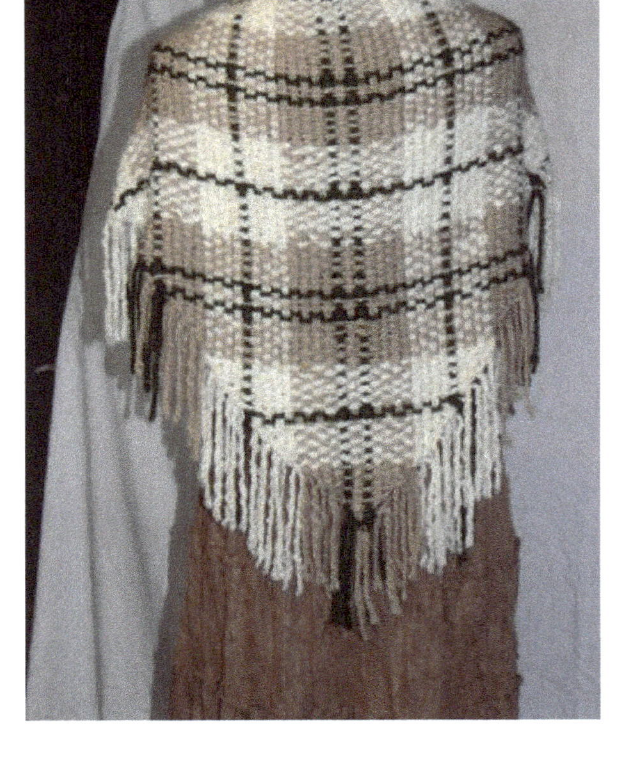

1	2	3	4	5	6	7	8	9	10	11	12	13	14	15	16	17	18	19	20
21	22	23	24	25	26	27	28	29	30	31	32	33	34	35	36	37	38	39	40
41	42	43	44	45	46	47	48	49	50	51	52	53	54	55	56	57	58	59	60
61																			

6ft Triangle Conversion

Approximate Yardage:

White: 135 yards
Green: 50 yards
Tan: 142 yards

Nail 1-2 (2 nails): White
Nail 3 (1 nail): Green
Nail 4-7 (4 nails): White
Nail 8-11 (4 nails): Tan
Nail 12 (1 nail): Green
Nail 13 (1 nail): Tan
Nail 14 (1 nail): Green
Nail 15-18 (4 nails): Tan
Nail 19-22 (4 nails): White

Repeat Nails 3-22 *three times*

Nail 63 (1 nail): Green
Nail 64-67 (4 nails): White
Nail 68-71 (4 nails): Tan
Nail 72 (1 nail): Green
Nail 73 (1 nail): Tan

Tie off slip knot and last woven strand.
Add any last minute embellishments (Fringe) and then pull off your loom.

1	2	3	4	5	6	7	8	9	10	11	12	13	14	15	16	17	18	19	20
21	22	23	24	25	26	27	28	29	30	31	32	33	34	35	36	37	38	39	40
41	42	43	44	45	46	47	48	49	50	51	52	53	54	55	56	57	58	59	60
61	62	63	64	65	66	67	68	69	70	71	72	73							

NEW

Difficulty: **

**Pattern 8.5 – Low Land Plaid
5ft Triangle**

Approximate Yardage:

Brown: 104 yards
Purple: 88 yards
White: 50 yards

Nail 1-2 (2 nails): Brown
Nail 3-4 (2 nails): Purple
Nail 5 (1 nail): White
Nail 6-7 (2 nails): Purple
Nail 8-10 (3 nails): Brown
Nail 11 (1 nail): White
Nail 12 (1 nail): Purple
Nail 13 (1 nail): White
Nail 14-16 (3 nails): Brown

Repeat Nails 3-16 *four times*

Nail 59-60 (2 nails): Purple
Nail 61 (1 nail): White

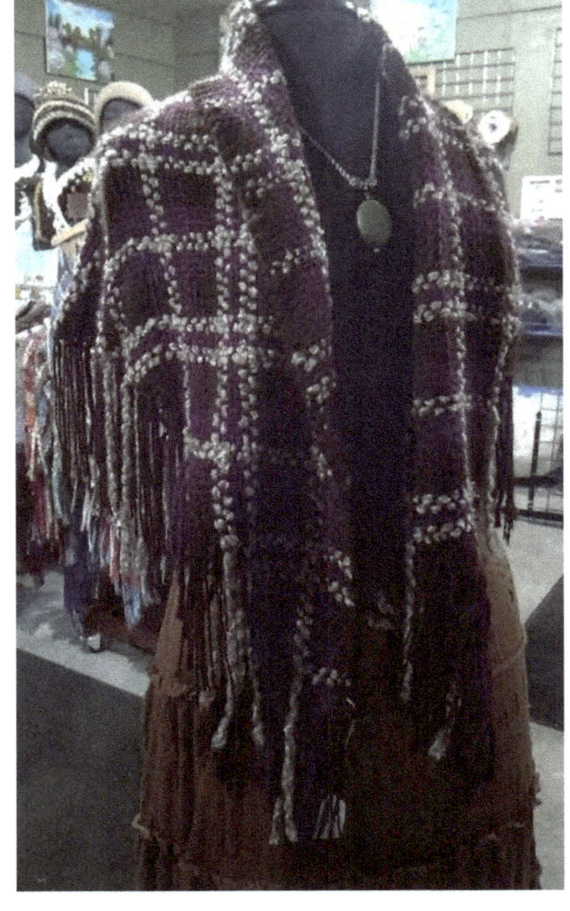

Tie off slip knot and last woven strand.
Add any last minute embellishments (Fringe) and then pull off your loom.

1	2	3	4	5	6	7	8	9	10	11	12	13	14	15	16	17	18	19	20
21	22	23	24	25	26	27	28	29	30	31	32	33	34	35	36	37	38	39	40
41	42	43	44	45	46	47	48	49	50	51	52	53	54	55	56	57	58	59	60
61																			

6ft Triangle Conversion

Approximate Yardage:

Brown: 135 yards
Purple: 122 yards
White: 70 yards

Nail 1-2 (2 nails): Purple
Nail 3 (1 nail): White
Nail 4-5 (2 nails): Purple
Nail 6-8 (3 nails): Brown
Nail 9 (1 nail): White
Nail 10 (1 nail): Purple
Nail 11 (1 nail): White
Nail 12-14 (3 nails): Brown

Repeat nails 1-14 *four times*

Nail 71-72 (2 nails): Purple
Nail 73 (1 nail): White

Tie off slip knot and last woven strand.
Add any last minute embellishments (Fringe) and then pull off your loom.

1	2	3	4	5	6	7	8	9	10	11	12	13	14	15	16	17	18	19	20
21	22	23	24	25	26	27	28	29	30	31	32	33	34	35	36	37	38	39	40
41	42	43	44	45	46	47	48	49	50	51	52	53	54	55	56	57	58	59	60
61	62	63	64	65	66	67	68	69	70	71	72	73							

Difficulty: ***

**Pattern 9– Muddy Pastures
5ft Triangle**

<u>Approximate Yardage:</u>

Dark Brown: 128 yards
Light Brown: 72 yards
Green: 44 yards

Nail 1-4 (4 nails): Dark Brown
Nail 5 (1 nail): Green
Nail 6-7 (2 nails): Light Brown
Nail 8-11 (4 nails): Dark Brown
Nail 12 (1 nail): Green
Nail 13 (1 nail): Light Brown
Nail 14 (1 nail): Green
Nail 15-18 (4 nails): Dark Brown
Nail 19-20 (2 nails): Light Brown

Repeat Nails 5-20 *twice*

Nail 53 (1 nail): Green
Nail 54-55 (2 nails): Light Brown
Nail 56-59 (4 nails): Dark Brown
Nail 60 (1 nail): Green
Nail 61 (1 nail): Light Brown

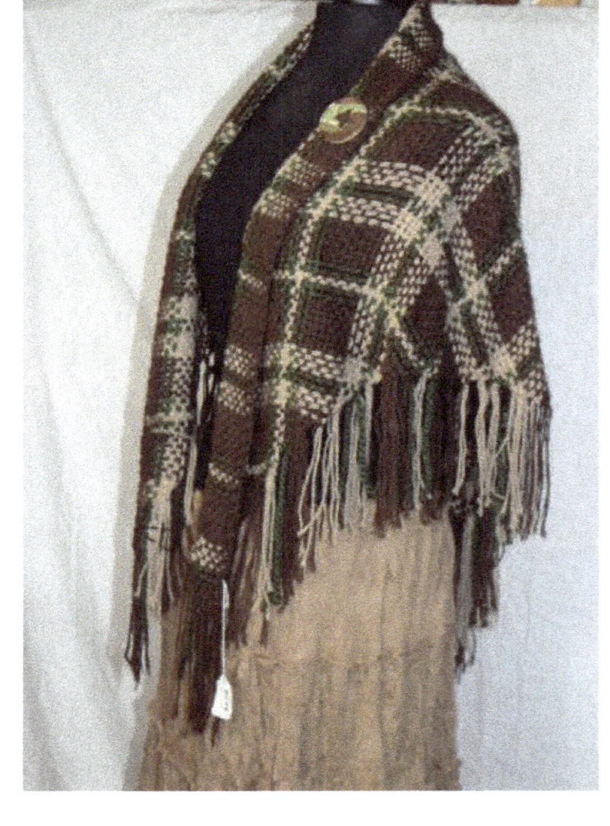

Tie off slip knot and last woven strand.
Add any last minute embellishments (Fringe) and then pull off your loom.

1	2	3	4	5	6	7	8	9	10	11	12	13	14	15	16	17	18	19	20
21	22	23	24	25	26	27	28	29	30	31	32	33	34	35	36	37	38	39	40
41	42	43	44	45	46	47	48	49	50	51	52	53	54	55	56	57	58	59	60
61																			

6ft Triangle Conversion

Approximate Yardage:

Dark Brown: 162 yards
Light Brown: 106 yards
Green: 54 yards

Nail 1-3 (3 nails): Light Brown
Nail 4-7 (4 nails): Dark Brown
Nail 8 (1 nail): Green
Nail 9 (1 nail): Light Brown
Nail 10 (1 nail): Green
Nail 11-14 (4 nails): Dark Brown
Nail 15-16 (2 nails): Light Brown
Nail 17 (1 nail): Green

Repeat Nail 2-17 *three times*

Nail 66-67 (2 nails): Light Brown
Nail 68-71 (4 nails): Dark Brown
Nail 72 (1 nail): Green
Nail 73 (1 nail): Light Brown

Tie off slip knot and last woven strand.
Add any last minute embellishments (Fringe) and then pull off your loom.

1	2	3	4	5	6	7	8	9	10	11	12	13	14	15	16	17	18	19	20
21	22	23	24	25	26	27	28	29	30	31	32	33	34	35	36	37	38	39	40
41	42	43	44	45	46	47	48	49	50	51	52	53	54	55	56	57	58	59	60
61	62	63	64	65	66	67	68	69	70	71	72	73							

Difficulty: ***

Pattern 10 – Autumn Magic
5ft Triangle

<u>Approximate Yardage:</u>

Black: 132 yards
Orange: 96 yards
Oatmeal: 14 yards

Nail 1-5 (5 nails): Black
Nail 6-11 (6 nails): Orange
Nail 12-15 (4 nails): Black
Nail 16 (1 nail): Oatmeal

Repeat Nails 2-16 *three times*

Tie off slip knot and last woven strand.
Add any last minute embellishments (Fringe)
and then pull off your loom.

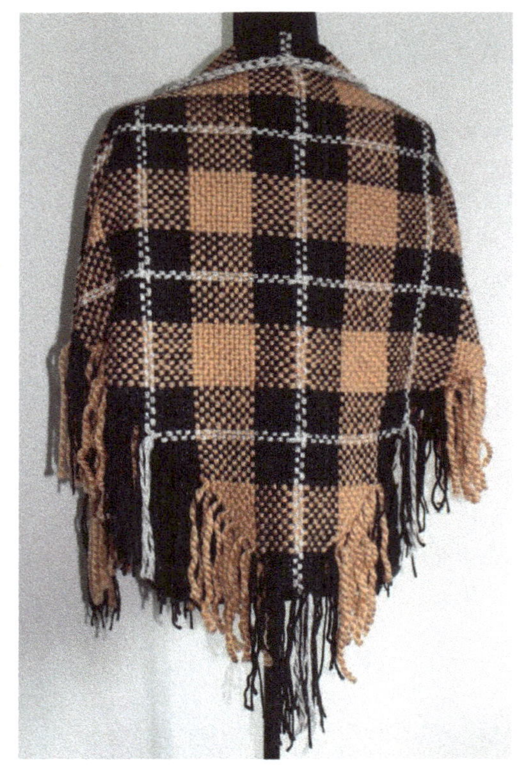

1	2	3	4	5	6	7	8	9	10	11	12	13	14	15	16	17	18	19	20
21	22	23	24	25	26	27	28	29	30	31	32	33	34	35	36	37	38	39	40
41	42	43	44	45	46	47	48	49	50	51	52	53	54	55	56	57	58	59	60
61																			

6ft Triangle Conversion

Approximate Yardage:

Black: 132 yards
Orange: 96 yards
Oatmeal: 14 yards

Nail 1-2 (2 nails): Black
Nail 3-8 (6 nails): Orange
Nail 9-12 (4 nails): Black
Nail 13 (1 nail): Oatmeal
Nail 14-17 (4 nails): Black

Repeat Nail 3-17 *three times*

Nail 63-68 (6 nails): Orange
Nail 69-72 (4 nails): Black
Nail 73 (1 nail): Oatmeal

Tie off slip knot and last woven strand.
Add any last minute embellishments (Fringe) and then pull off your loom.

1	2	3	4	5	6	7	8	9	10	11	12	13	14	15	16	17	18	19	20
21	22	23	24	25	26	27	28	29	30	31	32	33	34	35	36	37	38	39	40
41	42	43	44	45	46	47	48	49	50	51	52	53	54	55	56	57	58	59	60
61	62	63	64	65	66	67	68	69	70	71	72	73							

Difficulty: ***

**Pattern 11 – Over the Hills and Far Away
5ft Triangle**

Approximate Yardage:

Tan: 108 yards
Brown: 54 yards
Purple: 80 yards

Nail 1-3 (3 nails): Tan
Nail 4-6 (3 nails): Brown
Nail 7-9 (3 nails): Tan
Nail 10-14 (5 nails): Purple

Repeat Nails 1-14 *three times*

Nail 57-59 (3 nails): Tan
Nail 60-61 (2 nails): Brown

Tie off slip knot and last woven strand.
Add any last minute embellishments
(Fringe) and then pull off your loom.

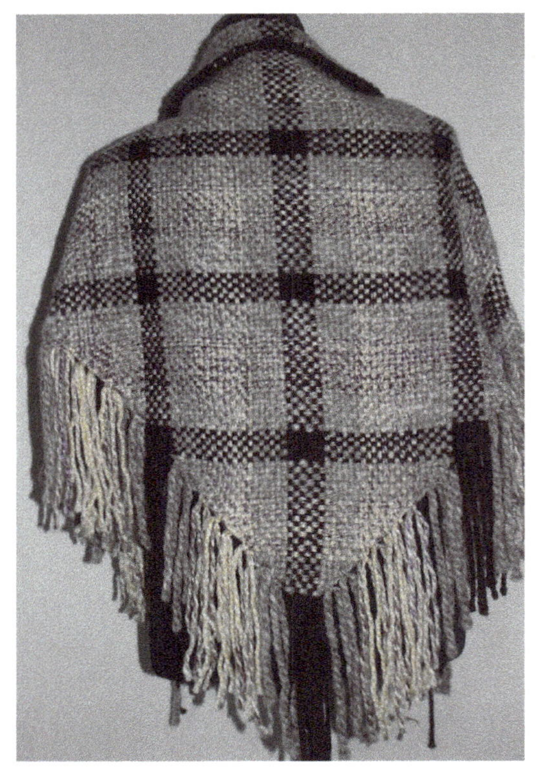

1	2	3	4	5	6	7	8	9	10	11	12	13	14	15	16	17	18	19	20
21	22	23	24	25	26	27	28	29	30	31	32	33	34	35	36	37	38	39	40
41	42	43	44	45	46	47	48	49	50	51	52	53	54	55	56	57	58	59	60
61																			

6ft Triangle Conversion

<u>Approximate Yardage:</u>

Tan: 135 yards
Brown: 79 yards
Purple: 113 yards

Nail 1-4 (4 nails): Brown
Nail 5-7 (3 nails): Tan
Nail 8-12 (5 nails): Purple
Nail 13-15 (3 nails): Tan

Repeat Nails 2-15 *four times*

Nail 72-73 (2 nails): Brown

Tie off slip knot and last woven strand.
Add any last minute embellishments (Fringe) and then pull off your loom.

1	2	3	4	5	6	7	8	9	10	11	12	13	14	15	16	17	18	19	20
21	22	23	24	25	26	27	28	29	30	31	32	33	34	35	36	37	38	39	40
41	42	43	44	45	46	47	48	49	50	51	52	53	54	55	56	57	58	59	60
61	62	63	64	65	66	67	68	69	70	71	72	73							

Difficulty: ***

Pattern 12
5ft Triangle – Oh my Cherry

<u>Approximate Yardage:</u>

Red: 180 yards
Black: 44 yards
White: 24 yards

Nail 1-5 (5 nails): Red
Nail 6-8 (3 nails): Black
Nail 9-14 (6 nails): Red
Nail 15 (1 nail): White
Nail 16 (1 nail): Red
Nail 17 (1 nail): White
Nail 18-23 (6 nails): Red

Repeat Nail 6-23 *twice*

Nail 60-61 (2 nails): Black

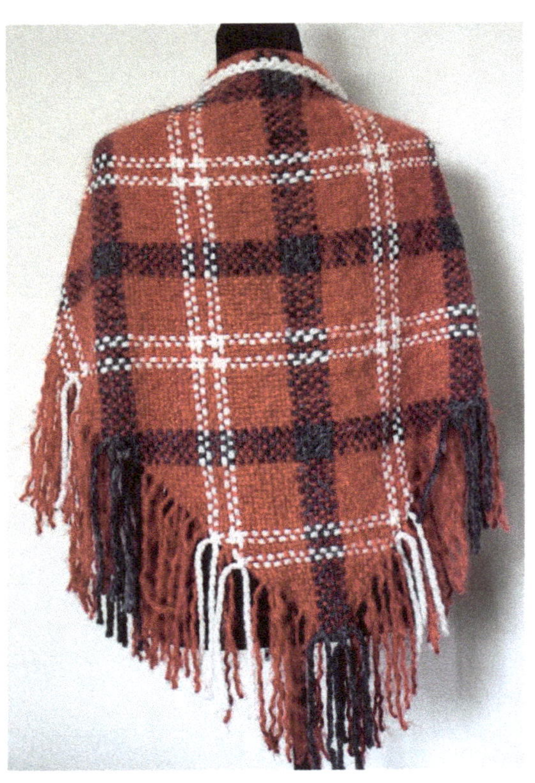

Tie off slip knot and last woven strand.
Add any last minute embellishments (Fringe) and then pull off your loom.

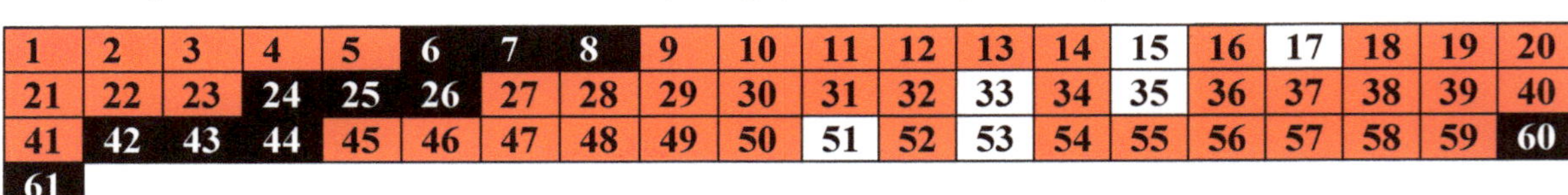

1	2	3	4	5	6	7	8	9	10	11	12	13	14	15	16	17	18	19	20
21	22	23	24	25	26	27	28	29	30	31	32	33	34	35	36	37	38	39	40
41	42	43	44	45	46	47	48	49	50	51	52	53	54	55	56	57	58	59	60
61																			

6ft Triangle Conversion

Approximate Yardage:

Red: 239 yards
Black: 48 yards
White: 36 yards

Nail 1-7 (7 nails): Red
Nail 8 (1 nail): White
Nail 9 (1 nail): Red
Nail 10 (1 nail): White
Nail 11-16 (6 nails): Red
Nail 17-19 (3 nails): Black

Repeat nails 2-19 *twice*

Nail 57-62 (6 nails): Red
Nail 63 (1 nail): White
Nail 64 (1 nail): Red
Nail 65 (1 nail): White
Nail 66-71 (6 nails): Red
Nail 72-73 (2 nails): Black

Tie off slip knot and last woven strand.
Add any last minute embellishments (Fringe) and then pull off your loom.

1	2	3	4	5	6	7	8	9	10	11	12	13	14	15	16	17	18	19	20
21	22	23	24	25	26	27	28	29	30	31	32	33	34	35	36	37	38	39	40
41	42	43	44	45	46	47	48	49	50	51	52	53	54	55	56	57	58	59	60
61	62	63	64	65	66	67	68	69	70	71	72	73							

Difficulty: **

**Pattern 13 – Shimmering Lagoon
5ft Triangle**

<u>Approx Yardage:</u>

Teal Blue: 44 yards
Gray: 92 yards
Blue/Gay: 104 yards

Nail 1-3 (3 nails): Teal Blue
Nail 4 (1 nail): Gray
Nail 5-7 (3 nails): Blue/Gray
Nail 8 (1 nail): Teal Blue
Nail 9-15 (7 nails): Gray
Nail 16 (1 nail): Teal Blue
Nail 17-26 (10 nails): Blue/Gray
Nail 27 (1 nail): Teal Blue
Nail 28-32 (5 nails): Gray

Repeat Nail 2-3 *once*

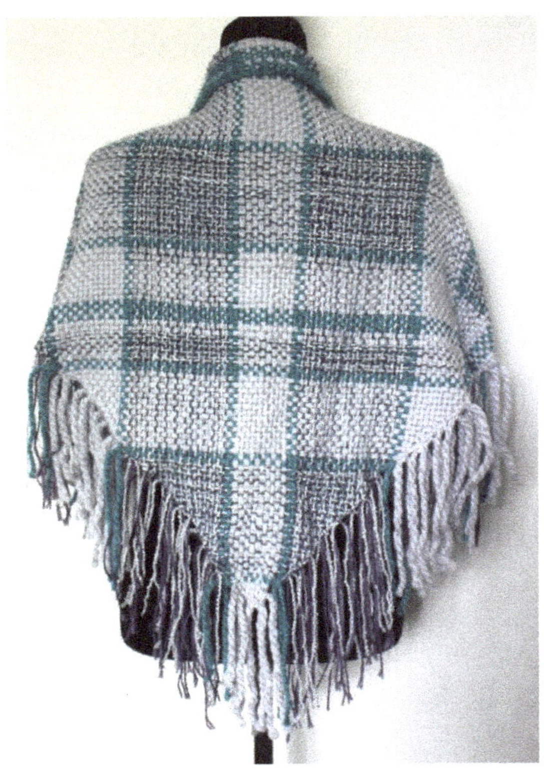

Tie off slip knot and last woven strand.
Add any last minute embellishments (Fringe) and then pull off your loom.

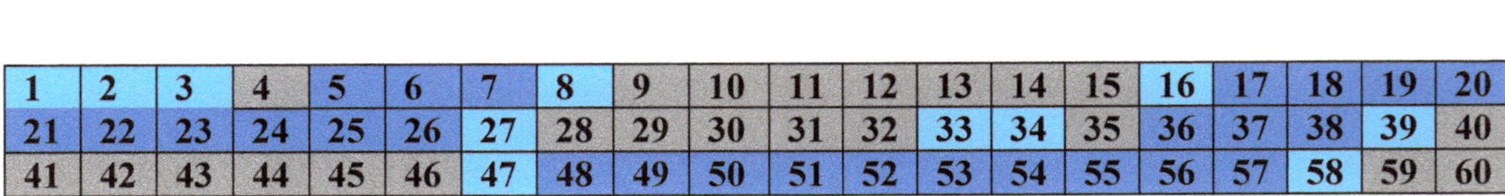

1	2	3	4	5	6	7	8	9	10	11	12	13	14	15	16	17	18	19	20
21	22	23	24	25	26	27	28	29	30	31	32	33	34	35	36	37	38	39	40
41	42	43	44	45	46	47	48	49	50	51	52	53	54	55	56	57	58	59	60

6ft Triangle Conversion

<u>Approximate Yardage:</u>

Gray: 126 yards
Blue: 149 yards
Black: 54 yards

Nail 1-6 (6 nails): Blue
Nail 7-8 (2 nails): Black
Nail 9 (1 nail): Blue
Nail 10-12 (3 nails): Gray
Nail 13 (1 nail): Black
Nail 14-20 (7 nails): Blue
Nail 21(1 nail): Black
Nail 22-31(10 nails): Gray
Nail 32 (1 nail): Black

Repeat Nail 2-32 *once*

Nail 64-68 (5 nails): Blue
Nail 69 (1 nail): Black
Nail 71(1 nail): Blue
Nail 72-73 (2 nails): Gray

Tie off slip knot and last woven strand.
Add any last minute embellishments (Fringe) and then pull off your loom.

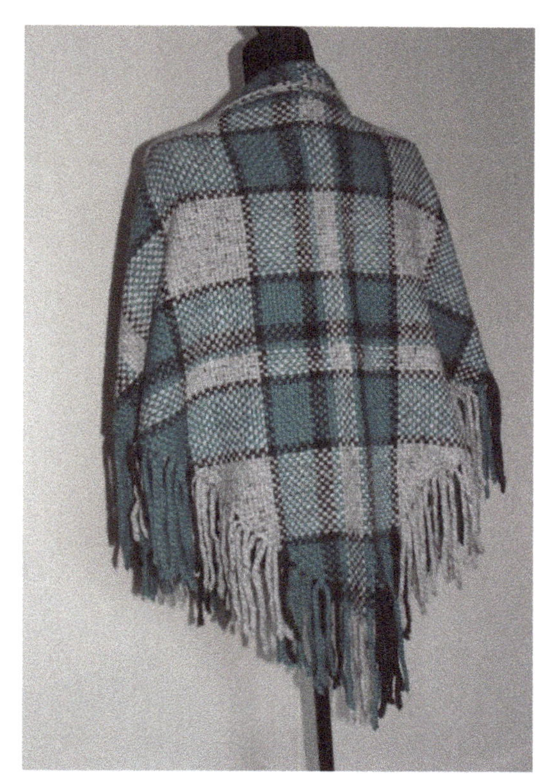

1	2	3	4	5	6	7	8	9	10	11	12	13	14	15	16	17	18	19	20
21	22	23	24	25	26	27	28	29	30	31	32	33	34	35	36	37	38	39	40
41	42	43	44	45	46	47	48	49	50	51	52	53	54	55	56	57	58	59	60
61	62	63	64	65	66	67	68	69	70	71	72	73							

Difficulty: **

**Pattern 14 – Frosty Sky's and Rosie Cheeks
5ft Triangle**

Approximate Yardage:

Tan: 172 yards
Purple: 54 yards
Gray: 16 yards

Nail 1-3 (3 nails): Tan
Nail 4-6 (3 nails): Purple
Nail 7-11 (5 nails): Tan
Nail 12 (1 nail): Gray
Nail 13-17 (5 nails): Tan

Repeat Nail 4-17 *three times*

Nail 60-61 (2 nails): Purple

Tie off slip knot and last woven strand.
Add any last minute embellishments
(Fringe) and then pull off your loom.

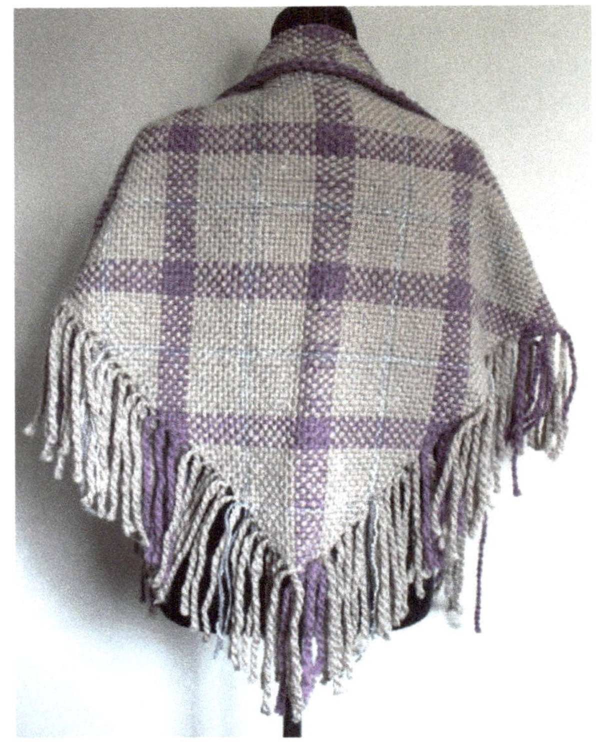

1	2	3	4	5	6	7	8	9	10	11	12	13	14	15	16	17	18	19	20
21	22	23	24	25	26	27	28	29	30	31	32	33	34	35	36	37	38	39	40
41	42	43	44	45	46	47	48	49	50	51	52	53	54	55	56	57	58	59	60
61																			

6ft Triangle Conversion

<u>Approximate Yardage:</u>

Tan: 225 yards
Purple: 79 yards
Gray: 23 yards

Nail 1-4 (4 nails): Purple
Nail 5-9 (5 nails): Tan
Nail 10 (1 nail): Gray
Nail 11-15 (5 nails): Tan

Repeat nails 2-15 *four times*

Nail 72-73 (2 nails): Purple

Tie off slip knot and last woven strand.
Add any last minute embellishments (Fringe) and then pull off your loom.

1	2	3	4	5	6	7	8	9	10	11	12	13	14	15	16	17	18	19	20
21	22	23	24	25	26	27	28	29	30	31	32	33	34	35	36	37	38	39	40
41	42	43	44	45	46	47	48	49	50	51	52	53	54	55	56	57	58	59	60
61	62	63	64	65	66	67	68	69	70	71	72	73							

Four Color Projects

Difficulty: ****

**Pattern 15 – Under the Sea
5ft Triangle**

<u>Approximate Yardage:</u>

White: 100 yards
Dark Blue: 64 yards
Gray: 64 yards
Bright Blue: 16 yards

Nail 1-4 (4 nails): White
Nail 5-6 (2 nails): Dark Blue
Nail 7-10 (4 nails): Gray
Nail 11-12 (2 nails): Dark Blue
Nail 13-15 (3 nails): White
Nail 16 (1 nail): Bright Blue

Repeat Nail 2-16 *three times*

Tie off slip knot and last woven strand.
Add any last minute embellishments (Fringe) and then pull off your loom.

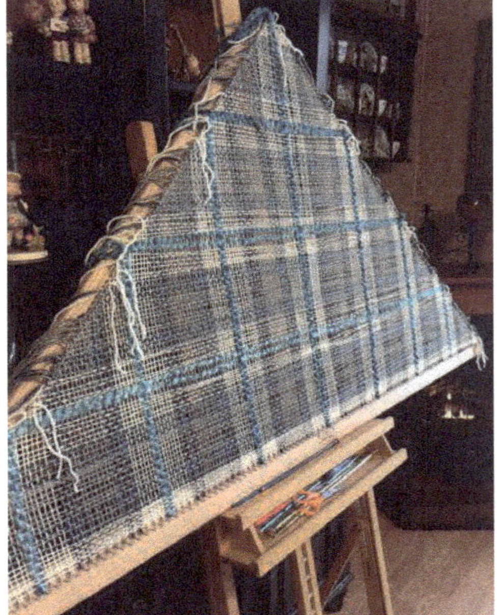

1	2	3	4	5	6	7	8	9	10	11	12	13	14	15	16	17	18	19	20
21	22	23	24	25	26	27	28	29	30	31	32	33	34	35	36	37	38	39	40
41	42	43	44	45	46	47	48	49	50	51	52	53	54	55	56	57	58	59	60
61																			

6ft Triangle Conversion

Approximate Yardage:

White: 122 yards
Dark Blue: 95 yards
Gray: 90 yards
Bright Blue: 21 yards

Nail 1-3 (3 nails): Dark Blue
Nail 4-7 (4 nails): Gray
Nail 8-9 (2 nails): Dark Blue
Nail 10-12 (3 nails): White
Nail 13 (1 nail): Bright Blue
Nail 14-16 (3 nails): White

Repeat Nails 2-16 *three times*

Nail 62-63 (2 nails): Dark Blue
Nail 64-67 (4 nails): Gray
Nail 68-69 (2 nails): Dark Blue
Nail 70-72 (3 nails): White
Nail 73 (1 nail): Bright Blue

Tie off slip knot and last woven strand.
Add any last minute embellishments (Fringe) and then pull off your loom.

1	2	3	4	5	6	7	8	9	10	11	12	13	14	15	16	17	18	19	20
21	22	23	24	25	26	27	28	29	30	31	32	33	34	35	36	37	38	39	40
41	42	43	44	45	46	47	48	49	50	51	52	53	54	55	56	57	58	59	60
61	62	63	64	65	66	67	68	69	70	71	72	73							

Difficulty: ****

**Pattern 16– Earth and Sky
5ft Triangle**

<u>Approximate Yardage:</u>

Tan: 68 yards
White: 64 yards
Blue: 96 yards
Blue/Tan: 14 yards

Nail 1-3 (3 nails): Tan
Nail 4-5 (2 nails): White
Nail 6-11 (6 nails): Blue
Nail 12-13 (2 nails): White
Nail 14-15 (2 nails): Tan
Nail 16 (1 nail): Blue/Tan
Nail 17-18 (2 nails): Tan
Nail 19-20 (2 nails): White

Repeat Nail 6-20 *once*

Nail 51-56 (6 nails): Blue
Nail 57-58 (2 nails): White
Nail 59-60 (2 nails): Tan
Nail 61 (1 nail): Blue/Tan

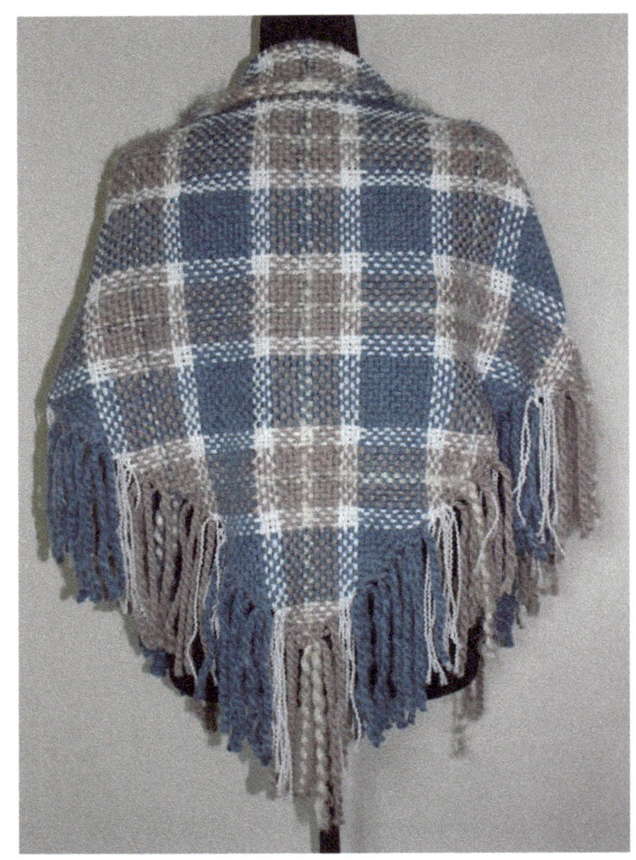

Tie off slip knot and last woven strand.
Add any last minute embellishments (Fringe) and then pull off your loom.

1	2	3	4	5	6	7	8	9	10	11	12	13	14	15	16	17	18	19	20
21	22	23	24	25	26	27	28	29	30	31	32	33	34	35	36	37	38	39	40
41	42	43	44	45	46	47	48	49	50	51	52	53	54	55	56	57	58	59	60
61																			

6ft Triangle Conversion

Approximate Yardage:

Tan: 81 yards
White: 90 yards
Blue: 135 yards
Blue/Tan: 21 yards

Nail 1-2 (2 nails): White
Nail 3-8 (6 nails): Blue
Nail 9-10 (2 nails): White
Nail 11-12 (2 nails): Tan
Nail 13 (1 nail): Blue/Tan
Nail 14-15 (2 nails): Tan

Repeat 1-15 *three times*

Nail 61-62 (2 nails): White
Nail 63-68 (6 nails): Blue
Nail 69-70 (2 nails): White
Nail 71-72 (2 nails): Tan
Nail 73 (1 nail): Blue/Tan

Tie off slip knot and last woven strand.
Add any last minute embellishments (Fringe) and then pull off your loom.

1	2	3	4	5	6	7	8	9	10	11	12	13	14	15	16	17	18	19	20
21	22	23	24	25	26	27	28	29	30	31	32	33	34	35	36	37	38	39	40
41	42	43	44	45	46	47	48	49	50	51	52	53	54	55	56	57	58	59	60
61	62	63	64	65	66	67	68	69	70	71	72	73							

Difficulty: ****

**Pattern 17 – Royal Petunia
5ft Triangle**

Approximate Yardage:

Black – 68 yards
Purple – 96 yards
Gray – 64 yards
Cream – 14 yards

Nail 1-3 (3 nails): Black
Nail 4-6 (3 nails): Purple
Nail 7-10 (4 nails): Gray
Nail 11-13 (3 nails): Purple
Nail 14-15 (2 nails): Black
Nail 16 (1 nail): Cream

Repeat Nail 2-16 *three times*

Tie off slip knot and last woven strand.
Add any last minute embellishments
(Fringe) and then pull off your loom.

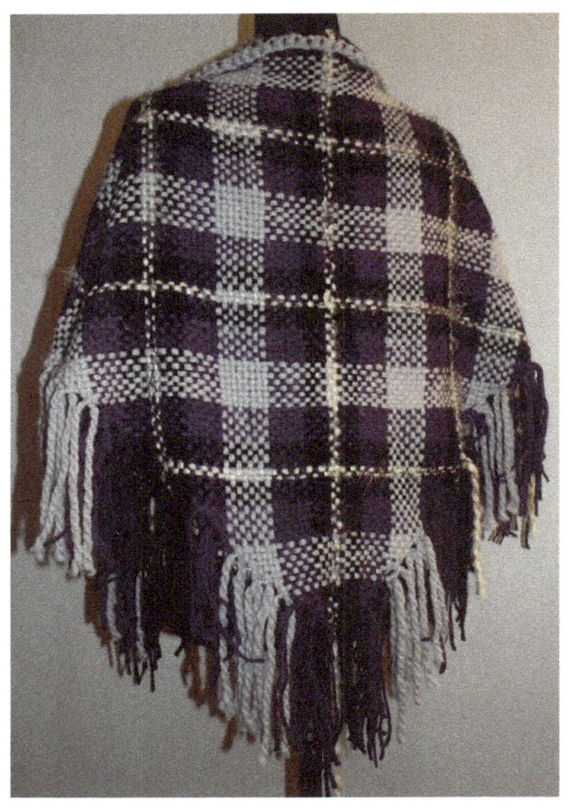

1 (Black)	2 (Black)	3 (Black)	4 (Purple)	5 (Purple)	6 (Purple)	7 (Gray)	8 (Gray)	9 (Gray)	10 (Gray)	11 (Purple)	12 (Purple)	13 (Purple)	14 (Black)	15 (Black)	16 (Cream)	17 (Black)	18 (Black)	19 (Purple)	20 (Purple)
21 (Purple)	22 (Gray)	23 (Gray)	24 (Gray)	25 (Gray)	26 (Purple)	27 (Purple)	28 (Purple)	29 (Black)	30 (Black)	31 (Cream)	32 (Black)	33 (Black)	34 (Purple)	35 (Purple)	36 (Purple)	37 (Gray)	38 (Gray)	39 (Gray)	40 (Gray)
41 (Purple)	42 (Purple)	43 (Purple)	44 (Black)	45 (Black)	46 (Cream)	47 (Black)	48 (Black)	49 (Purple)	50 (Purple)	51 (Purple)	52 (Gray)	53 (Gray)	54 (Gray)	55 (Gray)	56 (Purple)	57 (Purple)	58 (Purple)	59 (Black)	60 (Black)
61 (Cream)																			

6ft Triangle Conversion

Approximate Yardage:

Black – 81 yards
Purple – 135 yards
Gray – 90 yards
Cream – 21 yards

Nail 1-3 (3 nails): Purple
Nail 4-7 (4 nails): Gray
Nail 8-10 (3 nails): Purple
Nail 11-12 (2 nails): Black
Nail 13 (1 nail): White
Nail 14-15 (2 nails): Black

Repeat 1-15 *three times*

Nail 61-63 (3 nails): Purple
Nail 64-67 (4 nails): Gray
Nail 68-70 (3 nails): Purple
Nail 71-72 (2 nails): Black
Nail 73 (1 nail): White

Tie off slip knot and last woven strand.
Add any last minute embellishments (Fringe) and then pull off your loom.

1	2	3	4	5	6	7	8	9	10	11	12	13	14	15	16	17	18	19	20
21	22	23	24	25	26	27	28	29	30	31	32	33	34	35	36	37	38	39	40
41	42	43	44	45	46	47	48	49	50	51	52	53	54	55	56	57	58	59	60
61	62	63	64	65	66	67	68	69	70	71	72	73							

NEW

Difficulty: ****

Pattern 17.5
5ft Triangle – A Day for Daydreams

Approximate Yardage:

Gray: 100 yards
White: 96 yards
Pink: 24 yards
Light Pink: 22 yards

Nail 1-5 (5 nails): Gray
Nail 6-7 (2 nails): Pink
Nail 8-11 (4 nails): Gray
Nail 12-16 (5 nails): White
Nail 17-18 (2 nails): Light Pink
Nail 19-23 (5 nails): White
Nail 24-27 (4 nails): Gray
Nail 28-29 (2 nails): Pink
Nail 30-33 (4 nails): Gray
Nail 34-28 (5 nails): White
Nail 39-40 (2 nails): Light Pink
Nail 41-45 (5 nails): White
Nail 46-49 (4 nails): Gray
Nail 50-51 (2 nails): Pink
Nail 52-55 (4 nails): Gray
Nail 56-59 (4 nails): White
Nail 60-61 (2 nails): Light Pink

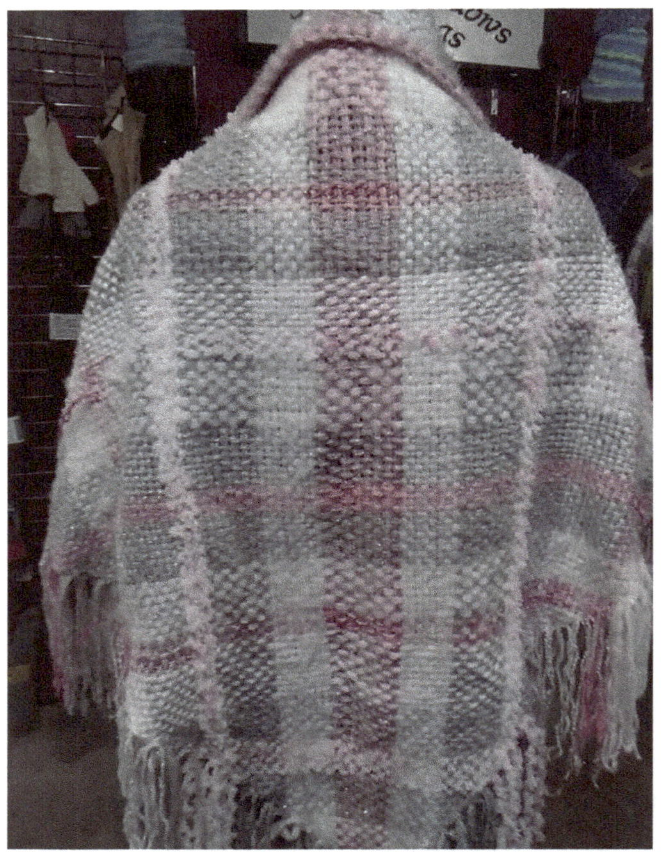

Tie off slip knot and last woven strand.
Add any last minute embellishments (Fringe) and then pull off your loom.

1	2	3	4	5	6	7	8	9	10	11	12	13	14	15	16	17	18	19	20
21	22	23	24	25	26	27	28	29	30	31	32	33	34	35	36	37	38	39	40
41	42	43	44	45	46	47	48	49	50	51	52	53	54	55	56	57	58	59	60
61																			

6ft Triangle Conversion

Approximate Yardage:

Gray: 117 yards
White: 149 yards
Pink: 27 yards
Light Pink: 34 yards

Nail 1-2 (2 nails): Gray
Nail 3-6 (4 nails): White
Nail 7-8 (2 nails): Light Pink
Nail 9-13 (5 nails): White
Nail 14-17 (4 nails): Gray
Nail 18-19 (2 nails): Pink
Nail 20-23 (4 nails): Gray
Nail 24-29 (5 nails): White
Nail 29-30 (2 nails): Light Pink
Nail 31-35 (5 nails): White
Nail 36-39 (4 nails): Gray
Nail 40-41 (2 nails): Pink
Nail 42-45 (4 nails): Gray
Nail 46-50 (5 nails): White
Nail 51-52 (2 nails): Light Pink
Nail 53-57 (5 nails): White
Nail 58-61 (4 nails): Gray
Nail 62-63 (2 nails): Pink
Nail 64-67 (4 nails): Gray
Nail 68-71 (4 nails): White
Nail 72-73 (2 nails): Light Pink

Tie off slip knot and last woven strand.
Add any last minute embellishments (Fringe) and then pull off your loom.

1	2	3	4	5	6	7	8	9	10	11	12	13	14	15	16	17	18	19	20
21	22	23	24	25	26	27	28	29	30	31	32	33	34	35	36	37	38	39	40
41	42	43	44	45	46	47	48	49	50	51	52	53	54	55	56	57	58	59	60
61	62	63	64	65	66	67	68	69	70	71	72	73							

Five Color Pattern

Difficulty: *****

Pattern 18 – True Loves Kiss
5ft Triangle

<u>Approximate Yardage:</u>

Gray: 84 yards
Textured White: 48 yards
Black: 84 yards
Shimmer White: 14 yards
Peach: 12 yards

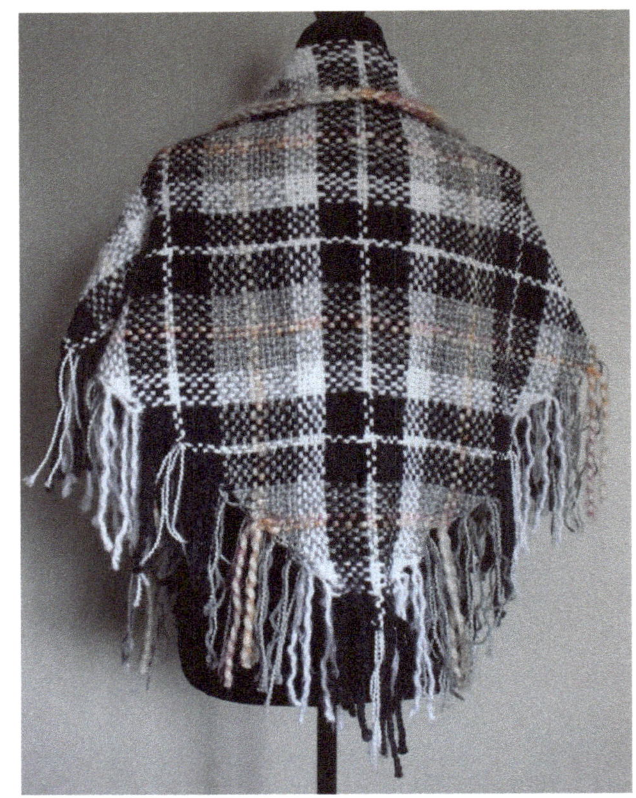

Nail 1-3 (3 nails): Gray
Nail 4-6 (3 nails): Textured White
Nail 7-9 (3 nails): Black
Nail 10 (1 nail): Shimmer White
Nail 11-13 (3 nails): Black
Nail 14-16 (3 nails): Gray
Nail 17 (1 nail): Peach

Repeat Nails 1-17 *twice*

Nail 52-54 (3 nails): Gray
Nail 55-57 (3 nails): Textured White
Nail 58-60 (3 nails): Black
Nail 61 (1 nail): Simmer White

Tie off slip knot and last woven strand.
Add any last minute embellishments (Fringe) and then pull off your loom.

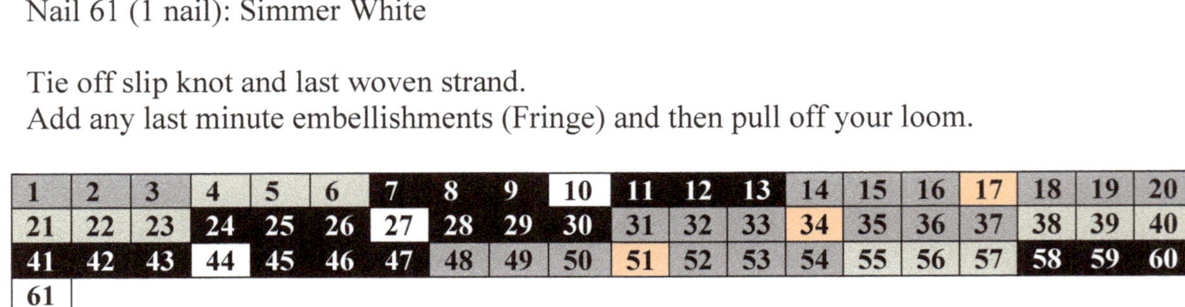

1	2	3	4	5	6	7	8	9	10	11	12	13	14	15	16	17	18	19	20
21	22	23	24	25	26	27	28	29	30	31	32	33	34	35	36	37	38	39	40
41	42	43	44	45	46	47	48	49	50	51	52	53	54	55	56	57	58	59	60
61																			

6ft Triangle Conversion

Approximate Yardage:

Gray: 108 yards
Textured White: 54 yards
Black: 126 yards
Shimmer White: 21 yards
Peach: 18 yards

Nail 1-4 (4 nails): Black
Nail 5 (1 nail): Shimmer White
Nail 6-8 (3 nails): Black
Nail 9-11 (3 nails): Gray
Nail 12 (1 nail): Peach
Nail 13-15 (3 nails): Gray
Nail 16-18 (3 nails): Textured White
Nail 19-21 (3 nails): Black

Repeat Nails 5-21 *three times*

Nail 73 (1 nail): Shimmer White

Tie off slip knot and last woven strand.
Add any last minute embellishments (Fringe) and then pull off your loom.

1	2	3	4	5	6	7	8	9	10	11	12	13	14	15	16	17	18	19	20
21	22	23	24	25	26	27	28	29	30	31	32	33	34	35	36	37	38	39	40
41	42	43	44	45	46	47	48	49	50	51	52	53	54	55	56	57	58	59	60
61	62	63	64	65	66	67	68	69	70	71	72	73							

Bonus Section!

We have been asked if shawls are the only things you can make on the 5ft loom. The answer is and will always be NO. You are only limited by your imagination!
In this section we provide you with a few different projects that are not shawls to try on the 5ft loom. But remember, this is not the only thing you can make on this loom!

Poncho

Weave two triangles of the same size. Lay one flat on top of the other and sew/crochet 1/3rd of the way across the long side (hypotenuse). Move the other side and repeat, leaving an opening in the center.

I'd crochet around the opening in the middle to make it more finished. Otherwise you now have a poncho to slip up and over your head.

Blanket

This is a nice project to move into putting more than one piece together. By crocheting or top stitching several 5ft triangles together you can make a decent size blanket.

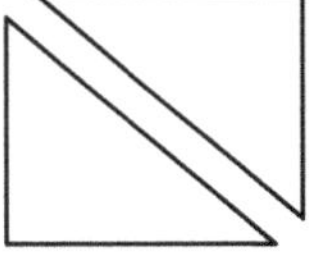

Right is two 5ft triangles with the hypotenuse (longest side) put together to create a square blanket. Or you can make a few squares to make a larger, rectangle blanket like the weaving four 5ft triangles and connecting them together, shown left.

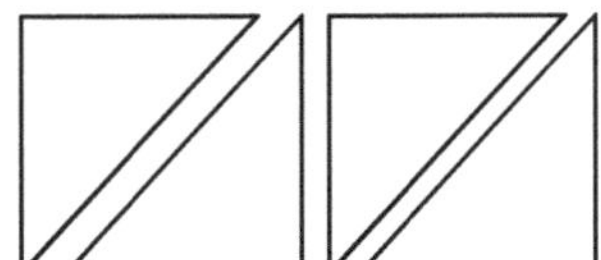

Scarf/Cowl

We touched on how to do this a little bit in the when you make a mistake section. When you are working on the 5ft triangle you can purposely stop weaving early. This leaves a bunch of string not filled in in the middle.

Instead of finishing the loom, get your scissors out. Very carefully cut the first 4 horizontal strings in the center of your loom. Now tie the two ends on the left together, effectively tying them off. Do the same to the right.

Repeat until you reach the end. After you have all the horizontal strings cut, make sure you've tied off your beginning ends. Now you can either add more fringe along the side or you can pull your projects off the loom.

You will have two separate triangles. You can now crochet or topstitch them together to make a new beautiful shape. Here is an example to the left. After crocheting them in this shape, take the two remaining short sides and crochet them together to make a neck cowl.

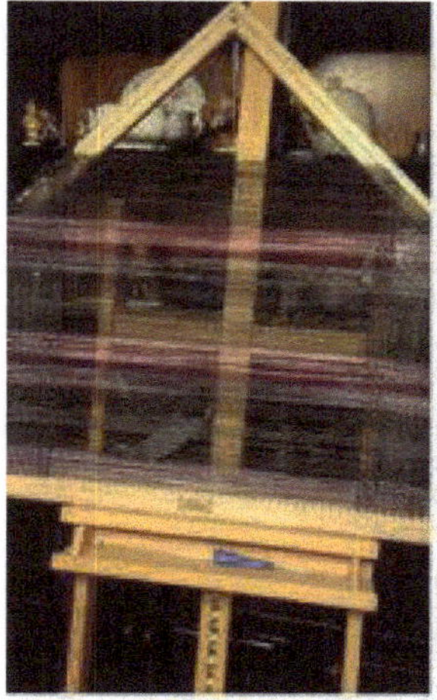
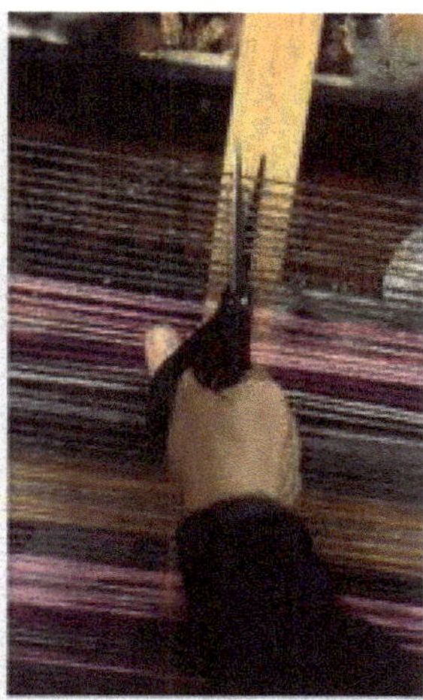
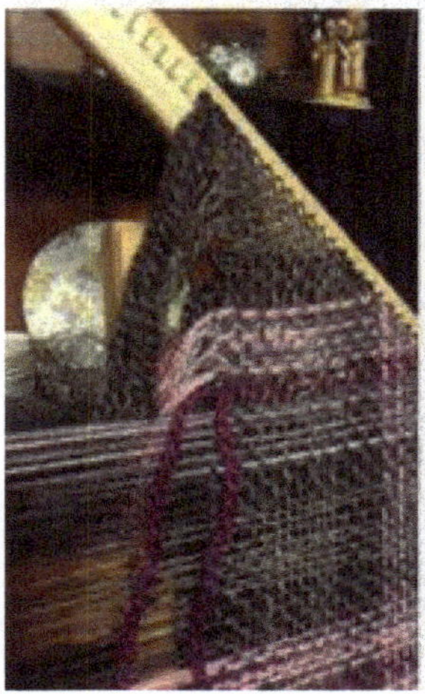
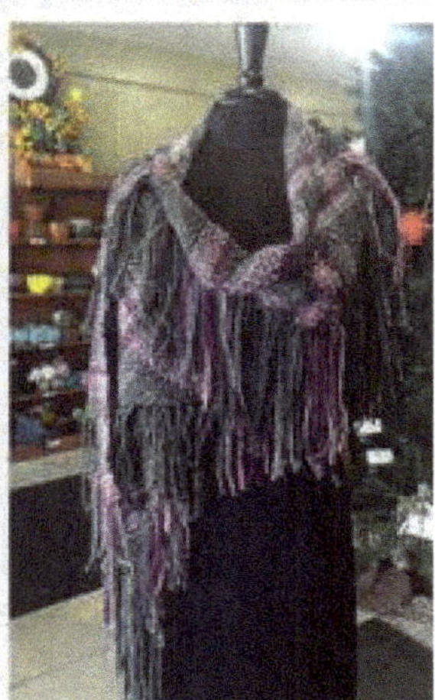

Tying a Slip Knot

A slip knot can be very tricky, but you can do it. We have provided you with an easy step by step guide with pictures to help you with the process.

Step 1: Start by finding the yarn you want to start your project with and find an end. I prefer to work with the 'wrong' end or the end that unravels around the skein of yarn. Other's prefer working with the end that pulls from the center of the skein. Start with whichever end you are comfortable with.

Step 2: Pull enough string out for fringe or enough to make you feel comfortable that is long enough for you to handle. You don't want it super long, just a comfortable amount of string. Approximately 12-16 inches will work nicely.

Step 3: Lay your string on a flat surface. Pick up the yarn closest to the skein and make a loop over near the end of your yarn.

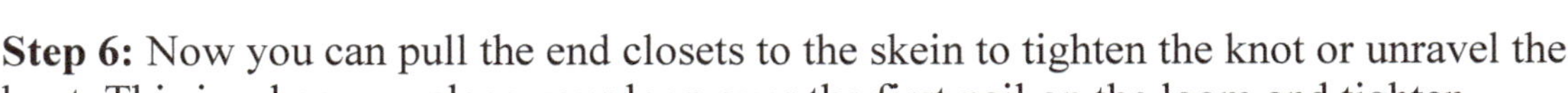

Step 4: Still holding the yarn closet to the skein, go under the loop you just made.

Step 5: Keep holding the yarn and with your other hand pull the end of your yarn until the slip knot forms.

Step 6: Now you can pull the end closets to the skein to tighten the knot or unravel the knot. This is when you place your loop over the first nail on the loom and tighten.

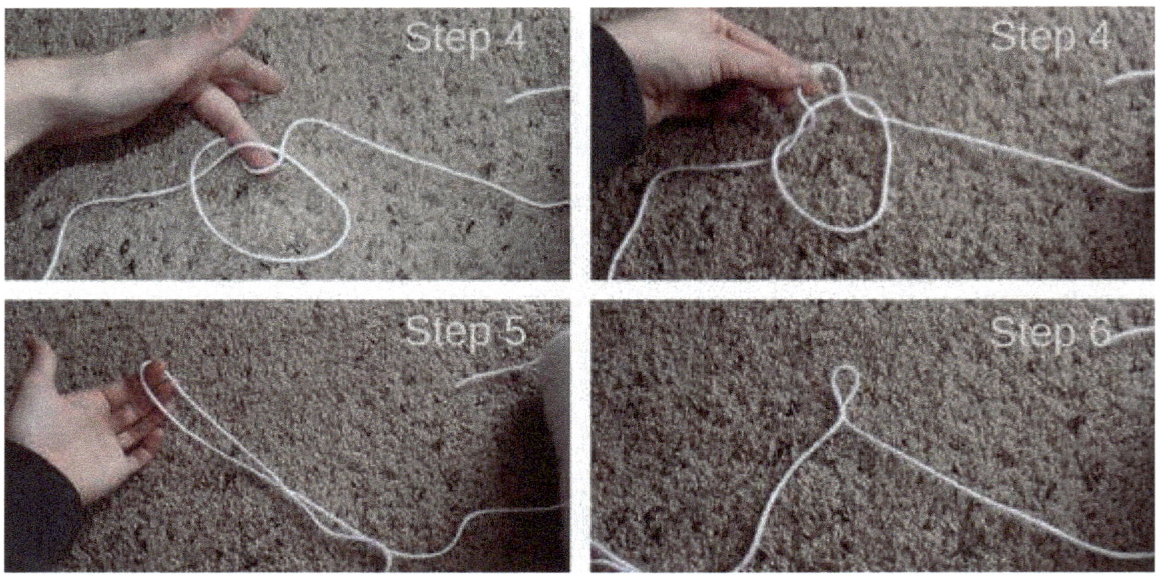

Reference

Looms and Yardage

*The yardage calculated is only for the loom and a simple border including fringe. Any other more complex border or embellishments will require more yardage. I have rounded my approximate yards up to make sure you have enough to finish your project. Our main goal is you buy enough yarn to complete your project with some left over.

Triangle Looms

6ft Triangle – approx. 400 yards
5ft Triangle – approx. 300 yards
4ft Triangle – approx. 250 yards
3ft Triangle – approx. 200 yards
2ft Triangle – approx. 150 yards
18in Triangle – approx. 100 yards
12in Triangle – approx. 80 yards

Rectangle Looms

21x63in Mobius Rectangle Loom – approx. 500 yards
10x60in Rectangle loom 10x60 – approx. 250 yards

Square looms

6x6 Square – approx. 100 yards
12x12 Square – approx. 200 yards
2ftx2ft Square – approx. 400 yards
4ftx4ft Square – approx. 800 yards

Flower Loom
Large Flower Loom

Meet the Authors

Theresa Jewell *Right, working on 2ft square loom

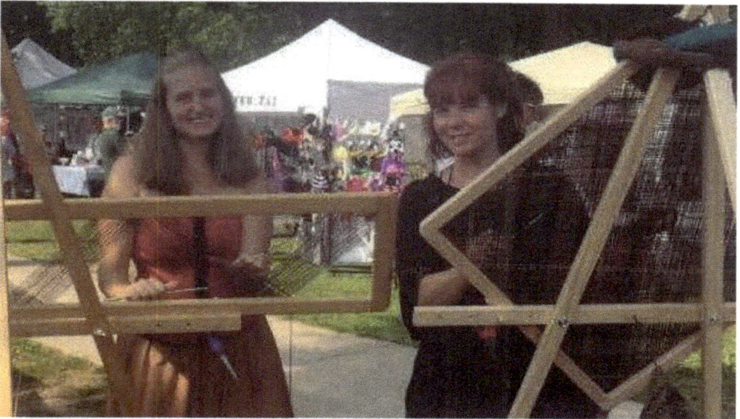

Co-Owner of Stone Mountain and Stoney Meadows Looms and Stoney Meadows Alpacas Farm with her husband Chuck Jewell. All the patterns found in this book are of Theresa's design, Ashli just helped her get them on paper.

Theresa is a self-taught yarn artist and has continued to learn and inspire others. Her knowledge of yarn crafts includes: spinning (2002), yarn dying (2002), frame loom weaving (2003), peg loom weaving (2009), tapestry loom weaving (2017), crochet, and felting.

Most days you can find Theresa at her farm taking care of her 'yarn babies' aka her alpaca or playing with yarn and coming up with more patterns to share in the next book.

Ashli Couch *Left, working on 10x60in rectangle loom

Owner of Bubbles 'n Stitches, her own little crafting business where she makes and sells all natural soaps and lotions along with all her woven items.

Ashli is self-taught in knitting (2011), all natural soaps (2014), lotions (2015), yarn dying (2017), and felting (2017). She learned spinning (2012), frame loom weaving (2012), and peg loom weaving (2017) from Theresa and will be learning tapestry loom weaving in 2018.

Most days you can find Ashli loading up on tea, weaving, making soap, appeasing her kitties, and working hard on the next weaving book with Theresa.

Meet the Maker
(Well, our LOOM maker)

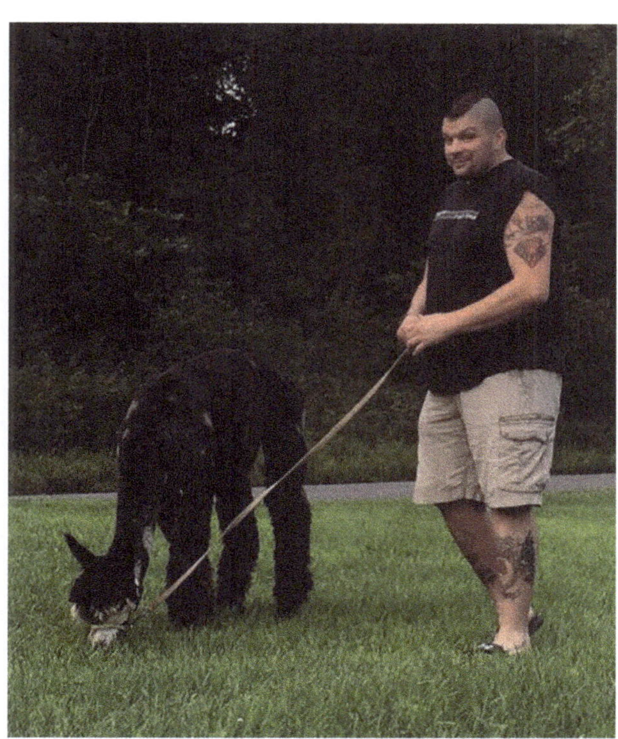

Chuck Jewell

Co-Owner of Stone Mountain Looms and Stoney Meadows Alpacas Farm with his wife Theresa Jewell. Chuck built all the looms showcased in this book.

Chuck was a professional kick boxer when he met Theresa and became involved with the farm. With no woodworking experience, he and Theresa purchased Stone Mountain Looms, received a crash course in making looms, and the rest is history. Since 2017, Chuck continues to improve his woodworking skills by creating new shaped looms for Theresa and occasionally Ashli.